EDMONDS-WOODWAY HIGH SCH

P9-CAA-530

86106297   972.91 DUN
Thirteen days of tension : the

THIRTEEN DAYS OF TENSION

The Cuban Missile Crisis

THIRTEEN DAYS OF TENSION

The Cuban Missile Crisis

LIBRARY
EDMONDS-WOODWAY HIGH SCHOOL
7600 212th ST. S.W.
EDMONDS, WA 98026-7553

ROSEN
PUBLISHING

Terri Kaye Duncan and
R. Conrad Stein

Published in 2021 by The Rosen Publishing Group, Inc.
29 East 21st Street, New York, NY 10010

Copyright © 2021 by The Rosen Publishing Group, Inc.
All rights reserved.

No part of this book may be reproduced by any means without the written permission of
the publisher.

Library of Congress Cataloging-in-Publication Data

Names: Duncan, Terri Kaye, author. | Stein, R. Conrad, author.
Title: Thirteen days of tension : the Cuban Missile Crisis / Terri Kaye
  Duncan and R. Conrad Stein.
Description: New York : Rosen Publishing, 2021 | Series: Movements and
  moments that changed America | Includes bibliographical references and
  index. | Grade level: 6-12.
Identifiers: LCCN 2019010207 | ISBN 9781725342187 (library bound) | ISBN
  9781725342170 (pbk.)
Subjects: LCSH: Cuban Missile Crisis, 1962—Juvenile literature.
Classification: LCC E841 .D86 2021 | DDC 972.9106/4—dc23
LC record available at https://lccn.loc.gov/2019010207

Printed in China

Portions of this book originally appeared in *Cuban Missile Crisis: In the Shadow of Nuclear War.*

Photo Credits: Cover, pp. 3, 64 Corbis Historical/Getty Images; p. 7 John van Hasselt/
Corbis/Sygma/Getty Images; pp. 10, 11, 29, 31, 50, 76–77, 85, 87, 102 Bettmann/Getty
Images; p. 13 pablofdezr/Shutterstock.com; p. 16 Roger Viollet Collection/Getty Images;
pp. 22–23 Hulton Archive/Archive Photos/Getty Images; p. 25 Enslow Publishing; p. 26
Keussler/picturealliance/dpa/AP Images; p. 35 Heritage Images/Hulton Archive/Getty Images;
p. 40 Robert W. Kelley/The LIFE Picture Collection/Getty Images; p. 43 Fox Photos/Hulton
Archive/Getty Images; pp. 46–47 Miguel Vinas/AFP/Getty Images; p. 57 Universal History
Archive/Universal Images Group/Getty Images; p. 58 Fred Stein Archive/Archive Photos/
Getty Images; p. 65 Carl Mydans/The LIFE Picture Collection/Getty Images; p. 69 Hulton
Archive/Getty Images; p. 73 Keystone/Hulton Archive/Getty Images; p. 78 Bachrach/Archive
Photos/Getty Images; p. 82 ullstein bild/Getty Images; p. 93 Lynn Pelham/The LIFE Picture
Collection/Getty Images; pp. 96–97 Boston Globe/Getty Images; p. 99 Bob Gomel/The LIFE
Picture Collection/Getty Images; pp. 104–105 Anthony Behar/picturealliance/dpa/AP Images;
p. 108 Museum of Science and Industry, Chicago/Archive Photos/Getty Images; pp. 110–111
AFP/Getty Images; cover and interior pages banner graphic stockish/Shutterstock.com.

CPSIA Compliance Information: Batch #BSR20. For further information contact Rosen Publishing, New York, New York at 1-800-237-9932.

Find us on

CONTENTS

INTRODUCTION

In 2015, there were rumors. Then, in 2018, an official report from the Pentagon confirmed the rumors. Russia was developing the most powerful nuclear weapon on Earth. The Pentagon refers to the weapon as Kanyon. Russia calls it Ocean Multipurpose System Status-6.

According to reports, Kanyon is an intercontinental, nuclear-armed undersea autonomous torpedo. It is approximately 5.5 feet (1.7 meters) wide and 79 feet (24 m) long. The weapon has a range of more than 6,200 miles (9,978 kilometers) and reportedly can be submerged to a maximum depth of about 3,280 feet (1,000 m). It travels 100 knots, which is just over 115 miles (185 km) per hour. Kanyon has a 100-megaton thermonuclear payload. This is equivalent to 100,000,000 tons of the explosive TNT. In comparison, the bomb dropped by the United States on Hiroshima to end World War II had a payload of 16 kilotons or 16,000 tons of TNT. This means that Kanyon is approximately six thousand times more powerful than the atomic bomb used in 1945. The weapon is also designed to get past American missile defenses. Kanyon is twice as powerful as any nuclear weapon ever tested. It is a doomsday weapon.[1]

The mushroom cloud over Hiroshima, Japan, following the first atomic bomb attack at 8:16 a.m. on August 6, 1945, rose to more than 60,000 feet (18,288 meters) in about ten minutes.

Kanyon is designed for a launch from a nuclear submarine. Its intended target would be a large port city. If a weapon of this magnitude hit New York City, it is estimated that eight million people would die instantly. More than six million more would be injured. It would also generate an artificial tsunami that could spread radioactive contamination inland. The devastation would extend far beyond the city and well into the suburbs. Radioactive fallout could rain over the entire Northeast corridor of the United States. Contaminated areas would be off-limits to humans for as many as a hundred years.[2]

The existence of a nuclear weapon as powerful as Kanyon is scary. But unfathomably worse is learning that a nuclear war is imminent and that the use of doomsday weapons is looming. In October 1962, the United States faced such a reality. For thirteen days, the country teetered on the brink of a nuclear war with another world superpower, the Soviet Union. The event, referred at as the Cuban Missile Crisis by the United States, was a major Cold War confrontation that occurred when the Soviet Union secretly placed nuclear weapons on the small island of Cuba, which is located just 90 miles (145 km) off Florida's coast. The discovery of nuclear weapons so close to the American mainland led to a standoff between three countries and three political adversaries. It also brought the nations perilously close to nuclear war. While key leaders in the United States and the Soviet Union negotiated behind closed doors, people all over the world prepared for the worst. Was this to be the end of the world as they knew it?

 **1**

UNMISTAKABLE EVIDENCE

At 7:10 on the morning of October 14, 1962, an American spy plane, a Lockheed U-2 approached the island of Cuba. With its elongated wings, the U-2 soared at dizzying heights above the sea and land. The single seat, single engine airplane had been built specifically for the United States' Central Intelligence Agency (CIA). The aircraft carried US Air Force number 66675 on its tail. It was equipped with sensitive, state-of-the-art cameras and capable of in-flight refueling in order to photograph the activities of potential enemies.

Major Richard Stephen Heyser, an experienced air force pilot, flew the plane over the island of Cuba at an altitude of 72,500 feet (22,098 m). Heyser was a pilot with the 4028th Strategic Reconnaissance Squadron, 4080th Strategic Reconnaissance Wing, United States Air Force. He knew that his flight was dangerous. When the U-2 was first developed in the 1950s, it flew so high that enemy anti-aircraft guns and rockets could not shoot it down. Nor could hostile fighter planes attain the U-2's altitude to fire upon it. But recently developed anti-aircraft rockets were able to hit the U-2. Heyser wore a parachute strapped around his shoulders. However, bailing out in the thin air and freezing

President Kennedy thanked Major Richard S. Heyser (*third from left*) for his bravery in flying reconnaissance missions over Cuba to gather photographic evidence of the missile sites. Heyser was the first pilot to conduct such a dangerous mission over Cuba.

temperatures more than 72,000 feet (21,945.6 m) above sea level was risky. It was not known if a pilot could survive such a long parachute drop.

Heyser must have pondered over what would happen to him if he were captured on Cuban soil. The U-2 operation he flew was a violation of international law. Heyser was illegally penetrating the airspace above a sovereign nation. He could be brought to trial as a spy and maybe executed.

Prepare for Any Eventualities

This perilous U-2 flight was ordered by President John F. Kennedy. The American president worried about the activities of Soviet troops and engineers on the island nation.

Agents on the ground told Kennedy that many Soviets had recently been stationed on Cuba. Dozens of Soviet ships were seen entering and leaving Cuban ports. This was the height of the Cold War, a grim period of tension between the Soviet Union and the United States. Cuba lay less than a hundred miles from the shores of Florida. What were the Soviets doing there? Kennedy hoped that U-2 photographs would give him and his advisers a clue.

Along the western shores of Cuba, Major Heyser started his cameras. Despite the altitude at which he flew, his

Daily U-2 reconnaissance photos taken during the Cuban Missile Crisis showed just how quickly work was progressing at launch sites where the Soviet Union and Cuba were installing medium-range ballistic missiles.

cameras were so precise that they took pictures of objects as small as cars and trucks parked on the streets below. The photo run took approximately seven minutes. Heyser took 928 photos before exiting Cuban airspace. He landed at McCoy Air Force Base near Orlando, Florida. His mission, though dangerous, proved to be routine. Heyser described it as "a piece of cake, a milk run."[1]

The Union of Soviet Socialist Republics

The Union of Soviet Socialist Republics (USSR), also referred to as the Soviet Union, was formed in 1922 following a revolution and bitter civil war. The country initially consisted of Russia, Belorussia, Ukraine, and the Transcaucasian Republic (Armenia, Azerbaijan, and Georgia). By 1940, the USSR had grown to include fifteen countries.

The Communist Party controlled the USSR. At that time, it was the world's largest country and had a hundred distinct nationalities. The country was two and one-half times the size of the United States and occupied one-sixth of Earth's land surface.

In the late 1980s and early 1990s, the USSR experienced a period of dramatic political and economic changes. By 1991, the USSR was dissolved and individual countries gained independence. Russia was established at that time with Moscow as its capital.

An Explicit Threat

Film from the U-2 cameras was quickly developed and sent to experts for study. One team of experts was housed above a shabby-looking garage on K Street in Washington, DC. This was the National Photographic Interpretation Center (NPIC), headed by Arthur Lundahl. The NPIC operated

This map shows the fifteen nations that made up the USSR. The USSR was created in 1922 by Vladimir Lenin (1870–1924), founder of the Communist Party.

out of a garage because the agency wanted to disguise its activities from any possible Soviet spies.

At first, the Lundahl team saw little more than Soviet defensive missiles. These were rockets designed to shoot down enemy aircraft. The defensive missiles were recently unpacked from crates and were not yet operational. Still, the new missiles presented a threat. When ready, they could fire upon future U-2 flights. The presence of defensive missiles also meant the Soviet Union was serious about their intentions in Cuba—whatever those intentions were.

After further study, the NPIC experts discovered a series of shocking photos. Images showed six long narrow objects covered with canvas. To untrained eyes, the objects seemed to be no more than large, insignificant boxes. But the canvas-covered articles were the same length and width as Soviet intermediate-range ballistic missiles (IRBMs).

The warning signs presented by the U-2 pictures stunned the photo-analyzing group. A Soviet IRBM was designed to carry a nuclear warhead. It had sufficient range to reach Washington, DC, or New York City when launched from Cuba. Each IRBM with a nuclear-tipped warhead was capable of destroying an American city and killing millions of people.

Arthur Lundahl called his boss, Ray Cline, deputy director of the CIA. Monitoring the enemy was the CIA's primary mission. Lundahl knew he had important, even earthshaking news for the CIA. Over the phone, he thought about the turmoil this would cause "when you tell him [about the missiles]."[2]

"Him," was President John F. Kennedy. The man chosen to inform Kennedy of the discovery was McGeorge Bundy, a special assistant to the president. Bundy waited

Two Leaders, Two Different Lives

John F. "Jack" Kennedy was born on May 29, 1917, in Massachusetts to a wealthy Irish Catholic family. He graduated from Harvard University and joined the United States Navy. After military service, he was elected to the United States House of Representatives and later to the United States Senate. Kennedy was inaugurated as the thirty-fifth president on January 20, 1961, at the age of forty-three. He was assassinated in Dallas, Texas, on November 21, 1963.

Nikita Khrushchev was born in Kalinovka, Russia, on April 15, 1894. At fifteen years old, he began working at a factory. He joined the Communist Party in 1918 and fought in the Russian Revolution. After the war, he received a technical education. He also became active in the Communist Party. Khrushchev was elected to the Central Committee in 1934 and later to the Politburo. He became Premier of the Soviet Union in 1953 and served until he retired in October 1964. He died in 1971.

until Monday morning, October 16, to tell Kennedy the distressing news. He could have wakened Kennedy during the night, but chose not to do so.

Early in the morning of October 16, Bundy found the president still in his pajamas and reading a newspaper. He told him of the U-2 pictures. The president said, "He can't do this to me."[3]

"He" was the Soviet premier, Nikita Khrushchev.

Nikita Khrushchev, the leader of the USSR during the Cuban Missile Crisis, had visited the United States in 1959. At that time, he encouraged a peaceful coexistence between the US and the USSR.

October 16, 1962, marked the beginning of an event that would become known in the United States as the Cuban Missile Crisis. In the days to come, the world held its breath as Kennedy and Khrushchev dueled with words, threats, manipulations, and negotiations. Thousands of troops on all sides stood poised for war. Most frightening of all, hundreds of nuclear bombs and missile warheads were armed and made ready. No one knew exactly what would happen if such a vast arsenal of nuclear weapons were fired. Many scientists believed a nuclear exchange between the USSR and the United States would end life on Earth. With fear in their hearts, people of all nations watched the October 1962 struggle between two nuclear superpowers. It was an unforgettable episode in history that lasted for thirteen tension-filled days.

A DIFFICULT AND DANGEROUS TIME

Early in the morning of April 25, 1945, a platoon of about thirty-five American soldiers patrolled near the Elbe River south of Berlin, Germany. All had survived many months of bitter warfare. Now the war in Europe was coming to a close. In the countryside, German soldiers were surrendering in large numbers. For five years, Europe had been held in the grip of World War II. Finally, it seemed, the conflict was near the end.

The American officer leading the platoon spotted troops on the east side of the Elbe. The officer peered at the soldiers across the river through his binoculars. They did not appear to be German. From their uniforms, he determined the men on the far side of the Elbe were Soviet infantrymen.

This meant the fighting, at least in this one sector, was over. The Soviet Union and the United States were allies in the war against Nazi Germany. For many months, the US army had marched toward Germany from the west, while Soviet forces approached the enemy nation from the east. The Soviets and the Americans shouted and waved at one another. The relief every soldier felt was overwhelming.

Germany surrendered twelve days after the meeting on the Elbe. On September 2, 1945, Japan, an ally of Germany, signed surrender documents, but only after the United States dropped atomic bombs on two Japanese cities. World War II ended. The war, which began in Europe in 1939, was the bloodiest conflict in human history. An estimated fifty million to more than eighty million people died. Many of the deaths were civilians.

Sadly, the end of World War II saw the beginning of a new conflict—the Cold War. The Soviet Union and the United States fought what was often a war of words. Both states had large military forces and powerful economies. Journalists referred to the Soviet Union and the United States as the world's superpowers.

The Cold War Is in Fact a Real War

The USSR and the United States were guided by opposing economic philosophies. The Soviets believed in a Communist form of government. The word "Communism" comes from Latin and means "belonging to all." Under Communism, the government owns all large stores, factories, farms, and other businesses. The means of distributing food and other goods are in government hands also. The Americans operated under a free-enterprise system. That system allows individuals to own businesses and keep the profits (capital) earned by them. The free-enterprise economic structure is called capitalism.

The USSR was the world's leading Communist nation. The Soviets imposed Communism on Eastern European countries, such as Poland and Czechoslovakia. Those nations had little choice but to accept Communism because the Soviet army forced the system of government upon them. The USSR and the European Communist nations were called Iron Curtain countries. In 1949, a revolution

The Communist Manifesto

Karl Marx, a German philosopher, is considered to be the father of modern Communism. On February 21, 1848, he and his coauthor, Friedrich Engels, published a pamphlet, *The Communist Manifesto*, in London. The pamphlet outlined ten points vital to Communism. It also called for the workers of the world to unite and lead a revolution that would tear down the capitalist world.

Marx and Engel believed that capitalism led to a social class system. This class system led to the mistreatment of workers. In a pure Communist society, everyone would give according to ability and receive according to needs. The needs of the society would be put above and beyond the needs of individuals. Therefore, all private ownership would be abolished and the means of production would belong to the entire community.

succeeded in China, and that nation emerged with a Communist government. After 1949, China and the USSR were rivals and competed with each other to lead the Communist world.

During the Cold War, many Americans were very vocal about their opposition to Communism. Politicians gained favor with voters by accusing rivals as being "soft on Communism." One of the most famous anti-Communist crusaders was Joseph McCarthy (1908–1957), a senator from Wisconsin. In the early 1950s, McCarthy claimed he had discovered Communist spies holding key positions in the US government. The senator said that Communists and those who favored Communism operated in the State Department and even in the army. Critics claimed McCarthy was simply seeking fame and called his anti-Communist campaign a "witch hunt."

Military Situations

In June 1950, Communist North Korea invaded capitalistic South Korea. The United States sent troops to aid South Korean forces. Months after the initial invasion, China moved a large army into North Korea and fought the American-led forces. The Korean War lasted from 1950 until a cease-fire was put in place in 1953. The conflict was a "hot" chapter in the Cold War. As is true with most wars, Korea was a tragedy. The Americans suffered 36,574 deaths and more than 103,200 were wounded. As of April 2018, 7,704 American soldiers who fought in Korea were still unaccounted for by the Department of Defense.[1] While the true figure of Koreans killed in the war is not known, it is estimated that nearly five million Koreans died, ten percent of Korea's prewar population. Many of these were civilians.[2]

The Communist countries had different goals based on their own national interests. However, Americans saw little difference between a Soviet Communist, a Chinese Communist, or a North Korean Communist. Many Americans felt that all Communists sought world dominance. The Soviet people held similar negative feelings about capitalism and the United States.

Edmonds School Dist. 15
Edmonds-Woodway High Library

US soldiers dig trenches into a hill in Korea in 1952. During the Korean War period that officially lasted from June 27, 1950 to January 31, 1955, approximately 6.8 million American men and women served. This was the first military action of the Cold War.

In 1948, the city of West Berlin in Germany was an island of capitalism perched in a Communist-ruled land. According to the terms of a complicated post-World War II agreement, Germany was divided into eastern and western halves. The Soviet Union occupied East Germany while the United States and its allies reigned in West Germany. Berlin, too, was divided into eastern and western districts. Both East Berlin and West Berlin lay deep in East German territory.

On June 24, 1948, the Soviet Union closed all roads and train lines leading to West Berlin. The Soviets did not explain the sudden move. Clearly the road closures were Cold War manipulations. West Berlin held 2.5 million people. Cut off from supplies, the West Berliners would have to give up their status as a capitalistic city and join the Communist fold. President Harry S. Truman (1884–1972) defied the Soviets by ordering the Berlin Airlift. For the next eleven months, US Air Force planes flew supplies to West Berlin. Planes carried food, medicine, and even coal to heat apartments. Finally, on May 12, 1949, the Soviet Union ended its blockade.

Times of high tension were called "freezes" in the Cold War. Periods of relaxation, called "thaws," often set in after a crisis was resolved. The Berlin Airlift represented a freeze in the Cold War. Never did Soviet and American armies directly fight each other during the Cold War. Instead, the Cold War was characterized by heightened fear and tension during incidents such as the 1948 Berlin blockade.

On May 1, 1960, a major Cold War freeze was triggered by the flight of an American U-2 spy plane. President Dwight D. Eisenhower ordered a series of U-2 flights over Soviet territory. The president wanted to learn more about

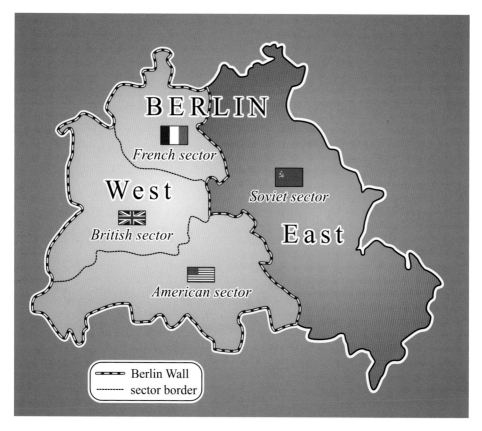

France, Britain, and the United States controlled West Berlin, while the Soviet Union ruled East Berlin.

Soviet progress in building long-range missiles. The U-2 aircraft was shot down by a newly developed Soviet missile. The pilot, Francis Gary Powers, managed to parachute out of his crippled aircraft but was captured. Soviet premier Nikita Khrushchev demanded an apology for this act of espionage. President Eisenhower admitted the U-2 was on a spying mission, but he refused to apologize. A Soviet court convicted Francis Gary Powers of espionage, and he spent twenty-one months in Soviet prisons before being released.

Tensions over the U-2 incident remained high when Premier Khrushchev met newly elected President Kennedy in Vienna, Austria, in June of 1961. Khrushchev demanded a final resolution of the Berlin situation. Kennedy refused to change the status in Berlin. At the time, many hundreds of East Berliners were fleeing Communism to become residents of West Berlin. To put a stop to these escapes, the Soviets built a long wall between the two Berlins. Berliners called it a *schandmauer*, meaning a "wall of shame."

In just two weeks, a temporary barbed wire and concrete block wall was constructed. From that point on, to get from

This photo shows construction workers building the Berlin Wall. On August 22, 1961, Ida Sickman died after attempting to jump from a fourth-floor apartment window in East Berlin to a West Berlin street below. She was the first person to die trying to cross the Berlin Wall.

The Fall of the Berlin Wall

The Berlin Wall was actually two walls separated by 160 yards (meters), an area referred to as a "death strip." The death strip had dogs, guard towers, floodlights, tripwires, anti-vehicle obstacles, and armed guards. The guards were under orders to shoot to kill. An additional barrier was built along the 850-mile (1,368-km) border between East and West Germany. This stretch contained more than one million land mines.

In June of 1987, the president of the United States, Ronald Reagan (1911–2004), gave a speech in which he proclaimed, "Mr. Gorbachev, tear down this wall!" While East Germans were permitted to begin crossing the border in November of 1989, actual demolition of the wall did not begin until the summer of 1990. It took two years to remove all border fortifications and an additional four years to take apart the barrier along the East–West German border.

East to West Berlin, travelers were required to pass through one of three checkpoints. East German soldiers screened diplomats and other officials before they could enter or leave. Other travelers were rarely permitted to cross the border. At least 171 people were killed trying to get over, under, or around the Berlin Wall before it came down.

AN ATMOSPHERE OF INTIMIDATION

Adding to the tensions of the Cold War was the deadly contest between the two superpowers to build destructive weapons. The United States was first to develop and use the atomic bomb, or A-bomb. An atomic bomb was dropped on the Japanese city of Hiroshima on August 6, 1945, and another on the city of Nagasaki three days later. The two bombs prompted Japanese leaders to surrender and finally end the war.

Numerous factors made the determination of casualties of the two bombings difficult. There was uncertainty of the population of the two cities prior to the bombings. Additionally, the bombs caused extensive destruction. Many bodies may have been burned in the fires that raged afterward. There was also utter chaos after the bombs were dropped. The Manhattan Engineer District, the code name for the secret US project set up in 1942 to develop the atomic bomb, estimated that approximately sixty-six thousand perished in Hiroshima while more than sixty-nine thousand suffered injuries. The bombing of Nagasaki is estimated to have left thirty-nine thousand dead and another twenty-five thousand injured.[1]

A Provocative Threat

In August 1949, the Soviet Union tested its first atomic bomb. Both Cold War rival nations labored to build more powerful A-bombs. In 1952, American scientists exploded a hydrogen bomb (H-bomb). It was many times more powerful than an atomic bomb. One year later, the Soviets developed their own H-bomb.

By devising more destructive bombs, the two sides achieved a balance of power. This balance meant that the Soviets and the Americans possessed arsenals powerful

The United States tested its first hydrogen bomb as part of Operation Ivy. It was tested on November 1, 1952, in the Marshall Islands located in the North Pacific Ocean.

enough to destroy each other many times over. Some writers and historians believed that the existence of the bombs actually prevented nuclear war, as one side was afraid of attacking the other for fear of being annihilated by a return strike. The nuclear bombs were weapons of indescribable terror. This standoff between the two nations was also called the balance of terror. Military generals had their own term for the vast arsenal of nuclear arms possessed by the two sides. The generals referred to the weapons balance as mutually assured destruction, often referred to by its initials: MAD. Since the word "mad" also means illogical, insane, and senseless, the reference was fitting.

Soviet nuclear weapons stirred up grave fears in the United States. Cities built nuclear bomb shelters where citizens could take refuge in case of an attack. Chicago's downtown bomb shelter doubled as an underground parking lot, which still serves the city today. Thousands of homeowners built family bomb shelters in their backyards. Plans for digging do-it-yourself shelters appeared in newspapers and magazines such as *Popular Mechanics*.

Government-issued movies and pamphlets advised Americans on how to protect themselves during an A-bomb attack. The first thing one would see in such an attack would be a bright flash in the sky. Upon seeing the flash, citizens were told to "duck and cover." This meant a person was to crouch down and cover up all exposed skin in order to shield oneself from the searing heat of the blast. Civilian defense agencies made a special cartoon, which appeared on television. A turtle danced into sight singing a happy tune that included the words "duck and cover." Then came a bright flash, and the turtle disappeared into his shell. Schools conducted A-bomb drills on a regular basis. At the command of a teacher, all students quickly ducked under their desks.

Even with drills and shelters, many experts predicted the true results of a massive A-bomb raid would be catastrophic. Blasts from atomic bombs release dangerous radiation that poisons the air and the soil. Radiation causes sickness and death long after the initial explosion. Even those who survived the first blasts would be exposed to

During duck-and-cover drills conducted in many schools, the teacher would scream, "Drop!" Students would then dive under their desks in order to practice what to do during an airstrike.

deadly radiation. In an all-out war between the USSR and the United States, hundreds and even thousands of bombs would detonate over the two countries. The radiation produced could destroy all life on Earth.

It was not known for certain if nuclear war would usher in doomsday and end life on the planet. But the doomsday possibility was real and the concept horrified the thinking of rational people. For billions of years, planet Earth had spawned life. Now, with one massive nuclear exchange between the two superpowers, Earth could be reduced to a dusty, lifeless ball speeding around the Sun.

How Would People React Today?

On January 13, 2018, a false missile alert in Hawaii sent waves of panic across the islands. At approximately 8:07 a.m., an employee of the state's Emergency Management Agency misunderstood that a drill was underway. He believed that a ballistic missile had been fired at Hawaii. He then sent out a warning to cellphones across the state. The message said, "Ballistic missile inbound to Hawaii. Seek immediate shelter. This is not a drill."

People feared for their lives and frantically sought shelter in homes and other areas. There was mass hysteria on the roads. Some said what they believed were final goodbyes to loved ones. Tourists did not have any idea of what was happening. It took 38 minutes to correct the message and reassure citizens of Hawaii that the message had been sent in error.

A Definite Threat to Peace

During the arms race, the two superpowers labored under a "never again" policy. Both the United States and the USSR were unprepared for World War II. When war broke out, they had poorly equipped and poorly trained armed forces. Consequently, the two countries suffered terrible early defeats. They vowed never again to be caught unready for armed conflict. The Soviets and the Americans poured money into their defense establishments. Their scientists worked to develop more efficient airplanes, rockets, and bombs.

Aircraft, specifically huge B-29 bombers, delivered the A-bombs that fell on Japan. During World War II, the piston engine B-29 was the pride of the American bomber fleet. In the Cold War, jet bombers such as the huge B-52 replaced piston-powered aircraft. However, jet aircraft, too, could be shot down, and scientists looked to missiles to deliver nuclear weapons.

The ultimate delivery system was the ballistic missile. Such missiles were launched into the sky and plunged downward at thousands of miles an hour. They follow a ballistic trajectory. This means the path of the missile is a large arc that is primarily determined by the speed of the launch and the force of gravity pulling it back down. Once the fuel that propels the missile burns off, it keeps moving. The path cannot be changed in flight. Eventually, gravity guides the missile to its target.

In the 1950s and early 1960s, no weapons existed that could destroy a ballistic missile in flight. Soviet and American scientists labored to develop huge long-range missiles, which were seen as the ultimate, unstoppable weapons of the Cold War.

The Modern Nuclear Force

Though the actual number of nuclear weapons in each country is a closely held national secret, it is known that the total number of nuclear forces worldwide has been reduced since the Cold War. In 1986, there were approximately 70,300. As of mid-2018, that number was down to 14,485. Though the number of nuclear weapons has decreased significantly, newer weapons are far more capable than those of the past.

Almost 93 percent of all nuclear warheads are owned by Russia and the United States. Each has roughly four thousand. Most other countries with nuclear arms only have a few hundred each. Additional countries with nuclear capability include France, China, the United Kingdom, Israel, Pakistan, India, and North Korea. All countries continue to modernize their nuclear weapons, indicating that they intend to retain them for the future.

The same rockets designed to shoot nuclear warheads at enemy nations could also be used to propel objects into space. On October 4, 1957, the Soviet Union shocked the world by launching *Sputnik I* into the heavens. *Sputnik* (a Russian word for "traveler") was the first human-made, Earth-orbiting vehicle. The satellite launch was a great scientific breakthrough, but even space was viewed as a competitive field in the rivalry between the Soviet Union and America. In Cold War terms, the Soviet Union had

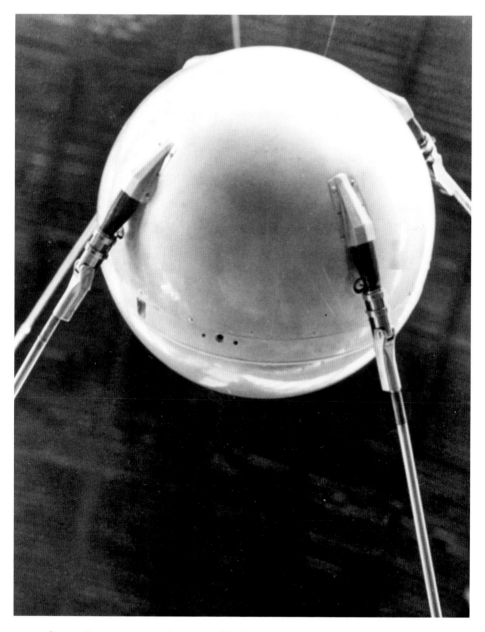

Sputnik was launched at 10:29 p.m. Moscow time from a launch base in the Kazakh Republic. It was only 23 inches (58.4 centimeters) in diameter but weighed almost 184 pounds (83.5 kilograms).

gained first place in the space race. Less than two years after *Sputnik*, another Soviet spacecraft, *Luna I*, zoomed past the moon. Early Soviet successes in the space race were bitter blows to American prestige. Finally, American scientists and engineers won the space race by sending men to the moon in July 1969.

Before the American success in space, however, another political issue demanded attention from the United States—the status of Cuba. In October 1962, the small island nation, so near to US shores, became a focal point in the most dangerous clash ever between the two nuclear superpowers.

CUBA: A SMALL NATION MAKES AN ENORMOUS DIFFERENCE IN WORLD AFFAIRS

The island that is now called Cuba was once a beautiful, lush area occupied by peaceful aboriginal groups. The native people called their home Cubanascan. However, when Christopher Columbus, an explorer sailing for the country of Spain, arrived in October 1492, the island was forever changed. Columbus called the island "Juana" in honor of the Prince Don Juan, the son of Spain's Queen Isabella. While the native people originally welcomed the new arrivals, they quickly realized that the Spanish had other intentions for their lovely island. Spanish invaders soon arrived, killing many with their weapons. They also brought with them diseases that caused the death of many others. Though the native people of Cuba resisted the occupation of their island, they had little chance in their battles against the Spaniards.

Cuba emerged as a naval hub for the great empire the Spaniards established in the Americas. That empire included present-day Mexico and extended into Central

America and South America. For three hundred years, the Spanish flag waved over its vast holdings. But in the 1820s, independence movements broke out in Mexico and South America. In less than a decade, Spain lost most of its possessions in the Western Hemisphere. Only Cuba and the island of Puerto Rico remained in the Spanish fold.

Independence movements began in Cuba also. The movements failed, but they instilled a spirit of liberty within the Cuban people. Cubans longed for the day when they would rise as a nation free of all foreign rule.

Cuba Matters

Early in its history, the United States sought to keep European powers from building colonies in the Western Hemisphere. Americans feared that such colonies could serve as military bases and threaten the United States. In 1823, President James Monroe (1758–1831) gave a famous speech to Congress, in which he announced the Monroe Doctrine. The Monroe Doctrine warned European nations to not establish military bases or other enclaves in the Americas.

Some American politicians viewed the Spanish presence in Cuba as a violation of the Monroe Doctrine. By 1895, a war for independence raged on the island. US President William McKinley (1843–1901) sent the battleship *Maine* to the port of Havana, Cuba, in 1898. The president hoped its presence would protect American citizens who lived in Cuba.

February 15, 1898, dawned a calm, peaceful day in Havana. Suddenly, a terrible explosion shook the port city. The *Maine* blew up and quickly sank in the waters of Havana Harbor. In the disaster, two hundred sixty American naval men lost their lives.[1] The cause of the explosion remains a mystery. While a fire, started by accident within the ship, may have triggered the terrible blast, other Americans claimed Spanish naval forces had blown up the *Maine* with an underwater mine. In April 1898, the US Congress declared war on Spain. The battle cry rang out: "Remember the *Maine!*"

The Spanish–American War was short and a decisive victory for the United States. A treaty signed on December 12, 1898, gave the United States control over Puerto Rico and Cuba, as well as the Philippines in the Pacific Ocean. Cuba was proclaimed an independent country in 1902, but the United States forced the new Cuban government to accept the Platt Amendment to its constitution. It said the United States could intervene and send forces to the island if future revolutionary warfare broke out. Also, the United States established and built a naval base on Cuban soil at Guantánamo Bay.

Cuban nationals called the Platt Amendment and the naval base examples of "Yankee imperialism." This form of imperialism occurs when Americans, sometimes called Yankees, intimidate their weaker Latin American neighbors.

American business interests bought land in newly independent Cuba and operated companies there. By the 1920s, foreign companies, many of which were owned by Americans, controlled 80 percent of the Cuban sugar industry.[2] Investors from the United States bought into the Cuban railroad system and owned electrical power companies. Tourism thrived as Americans and Europeans flocked to Cuba's marvelous beaches. US companies owned many of the best hotels and restaurants. The American

Guantánamo is technically a property rented by the United States from Cuba. The United States pays Cuba $4,085 rent annually. However, Cuba has refused to accept the money since 1959 to protest the US occupation there.[3]

mafia bought nightclubs in Havana and operated gambling casinos in the city.

The contrast between the lives of wealthy Americans and Cuban workers was glaring. Fruit pickers for the Boston-based United Fruit Company earned less than a dollar a day.[4] The pickers lived in tiny shacks. American employees of United Fruit resided in gated communities with swimming pools and golf courses. Cuban hotel employees, too, were underpaid. Foreign tourists spent more on a single meal than these workers earned in a week.

In 1933, an army sergeant named Fulgencio Batista (1901–1973) rose to power in Cuba. For most of the next twenty-five years, Batista controlled the country either as its president or as the power behind the presidency. Batista was a dictator, but American leaders favored him because he declared himself to be against Communism. To the people of Cuba, though, he was a corrupt and tyrannical leader. Under Batista's rule, Cuban citizens were tortured

Gitmo

The Guantánamo Bay Naval Station and the detention facilities, often referred to as "Gitmo," are located in southeastern Cuba on the corner of the Guantánamo Bay. The United States has officially leased the 45 square miles (117 square km) of land that the base sits on since 1903. The lease can only be terminated by mutual agreement. The area is mostly a Constitution-free zone. The lease states that Cuba retains "ultimate sovereignty" over the area but that the United States has "complete jurisdiction."

After the September 11, 2001 terrorist attacks, the detention center was repurposed to hold detainees in the "war on terror." However, it has also been used to house refugees from Haiti after a 1994 coup in that country. As of May 2018, there were forty detainees. Approximately six thousand people live on the base today. These include American military personnel, their families, and additional civilian staff.

and public executions occurred. The country's policies during his regime also widened the gap between the rich and the poor. Cubans felt betrayed by their government and overwhelmed by the influence of American dollars. They sought a hero who could lead them out of their despair.

Fidel Castro: Not Just Another Latin American Dictator

Fidel Castro was born August 13, 1926, near the town of Mayari, Cuba. His father was a Spanish immigrant who owned a fruit plantation. Fidel grew up in comfortable middle-class circumstances. As a young man, he attended law school, but revolutionary politics were his greatest passion. In 1953, he tried to overthrow the Batista government by leading an attack on the Moncada army barracks. The effort failed and Castro was sent to jail.

After serving two years in prison, Castro and his younger brother, Raúl, traveled to Mexico. The Castro brothers formed the 26th of July Movement, so named after the assault on the Moncada barracks that occurred on that date. In December 1956, Castro and his group boarded a small boat and sailed for Cuba.

Once on land, the men fought Batista's soldiers. Most of the revolutionaries were killed or captured. The Castro brothers and about a dozen others fled to the mountains to carry on the revolution. During this mountain exile, Castro became an exciting and dashing figure in the eyes of the Cuban people. He launched hit-and-run raids on Batista's forces. He broadcast revolutionary messages through a secret radio station.

On New Year's Day 1959, the 26th of July Movement triumphed. Castro and his men occupied Havana. Batista fled the country. At first, the American public cheered

Fidel Castro's full name was Fidel Alejandro Castro Ruz. He led Cuba for nearly five decades.

Castro's victory comparing him to Robin Hood, the folk hero of old England, who fought against a greedy king.

But while some American people admired Castro, the US government and American business interests were wary. Was Castro a Communist? Raúl Castro openly proclaimed Communist sympathies. Fidel Castro, at first, was more of a mystery. On a 1959 trip to the United States he declared, "We are against all kinds of dictators. . . . That is why we are against communism."[5]

Once he was in complete control over Cuba, Fidel Castro passed laws that broke up large plantations. Americans owned some of those plantations. Castro redistributed the plantation land to small Cuban farmers. Castro soon acted as a dictator himself.

By 1960, Castro had lost much of his popularity with the American people. His crackdown on political opponents within Cuba made him appear almost a bad as Batista had been. Also of concern was Castro's growing relationship with the Soviets. Key members of the Cuban government had traveled to the Soviet Union and conferred with Communist leaders.

Secretly, the US government launched plans to assassinate Fidel Castro. An attempt was made to lace one of Fidel's favorite cigars with a mind-altering drug that would make him sound incoherent during a radio address to the nation.[6] American authorities even contacted Florida gangsters, who knew Cuba well, to hire hit men and assassinate the Cuban leader.[7] The American people were unaware of these moves against Castro.

On April 17, 1961, an army of fourteen hundred Cuban exiles landed on the Bay of Pigs in southern Cuba.[8] These men were anti-Castro Cubans who had fled the island when he took power. They now returned in force to rally the people against Castro. At first, American leaders claimed they had nothing to do with this invasion. In truth, the CIA backed the operation. Its operatives recruited the men and trained them in hidden Central American bases.

The Bay of Pigs invasion was an utter failure. It had been planned under President Eisenhower. President

Operation Northwoods

Operation Northwoods, a top-secret operation proposed in March 1962 by the Joint Chiefs of Staff, was designed to justify US military action against Cuba. Using both overt and covert military operations, the US government would essentially trick the American people and the world into believing that a US attack against Cuba was necessary.

Suggested incidents included blowing up the ammunition on the base at Guantánamo Bay in order to start a fire. Another idea was to sink an American ship in the harbor. There would even be funerals for the mock-victims. Incidents would be blamed on Cuban saboteurs. It was suggested that a boatload of Cubans in route to Florida could be sunk. The incident could be real or simulated according to the plan. There was also a recommendation to stage a Cuban aircraft attacking and shooting down a chartered American plane in route from the United States to Jamaica.

A group of Cuban exiles are captured on April 20, 1961, by Castro's forces. During the Bay of Pigs invasion, 114 Cuban exiles were killed and more than 1,100 were taken prisoner. Most were freed twenty months later in exchange for $53 million in food and medical supplies from the United States to Cuba.

Kennedy inherited the operation when he took office early in 1961. The Kennedy team wanted to disguise American involvement in the attack and canceled much of the planned air support. Most members of the exile army were forced to surrender. Embarrassed, President Kennedy

finally admitted his government's role in the botched invasion. Kennedy said, "There's an old saying that victory has a hundred fathers and defeat is an orphan."[9]

Despite the Bay of Pigs disaster, John F. Kennedy was still determined to topple Fidel Castro. He ordered a series of top-secret covert actions designed to overthrow or even kill the Cuban leader.[10] Edward Lansdale, Special Operations Chief at the Pentagon, received the assignment to overthrow Fidel Castro. The mission was named Operation Mongoose. Lansdale was not permitted to engage US troops in combat during the operation.

Attorney General Robert Kennedy, the president's younger brother, put pressure on Lansdale to get results. In February 1962, Lansdale proposed a plan that would start in March and end in October with Castro's overthrow. The plan was to organize a rebellion within Cuba against Castro. It consisted of a coordinated program of political, psychological, military, sabotage, and intelligence operations. It also proposed assassination attempts against key political leaders in Cuba, including Castro.[11]

In December 1961, Castro declared he was a Communist and that he was building a Communist state in Cuba. Then, in July 1962, Raúl Castro, who served as Cuba's Defense Minister, visited the Soviet Union. During that visit, Nikita Khrushchev told the Castro brother that the USSR wanted to help Cuba defend its liberty and its sovereignty.

Khrushchev offered to put Soviet missiles on Cuban soil. The Soviet leader made the point that the presence of such missiles would deter the United States from any further invasions. The Castro government accepted the offer. This missile agreement, codenamed Anadyr, was made in strict secrecy between Cuba and the Soviet Union. The United States did not know that missiles were about to be placed on an island less than one hundred miles from American soil.

CLEAR AND PRESENT DANGER

At 9:00 a.m. on Tuesday, October 16, 1962, Robert Kennedy received an urgent call from his brother, President John F. Kennedy, asking him to come to the White House. He indicated that the United States may be in the midst of a crisis with the USSR.

The Cuban Missile Crisis Begins

At 11:45 a.m., an emergency meeting began in the White House. Vice President Lyndon Johnson was present as were President Kennedy and Robert Kennedy. Secretary of State Dean Rusk, Secretary of Defense Robert McNamara, US Army general Maxwell Taylor, United Nations ambassador Adlai Stevenson, and other high-ranking Kennedy advisers were in attendance as well. This morning meeting marked the beginning of the Cuban Missile Crisis, an event that would bring the United States to the brink of nuclear war.

Day One: Tuesday, October 16, 1962

Photo experts showed the Kennedy team pictures taken by the U-2 flight. The pictures revealed workers on the ground clearing a field. At first glance, the clearing

Robert Kennedy, the seventh child of nine born to Joseph and Rose Kennedy, was more than eight years younger than his brother, John F. Kennedy. He served as the sixty-fourth US Attorney General from January 1961 to September 1964.

looked insignificant, almost like a football field. But the experts insisted it would be used to construct a missile-launching site. Small rectangular shapes seen near the field were the actual rocket launchers. The people who interpreted the photos concluded that the missiles would be ready for firing in about ten days.

The weapons being installed were medium range ballistic missiles (MRBMs), with a range of about 600 to 1,900 miles (970 to 3,060 km), and intermediate range ballistic missiles (IRBMs), with a range of about 1,900 to 3,100 miles (3,060 to 5,000 km). Much larger intercontinental ballistic missiles (ICBMs) had ranges of more than 3,100 miles (5,000 km). During the presidential campaign of 1960, then-candidate Kennedy complained the nation had fallen into a "missile gap" in its competition with the Soviets. However, this so-called gap simply did not exist. In late 1962, the United States had far more ICBMs than the Soviets.[1] Kennedy and his team believed the Soviet deployment was Khrushchev's way of equalizing the nuclear balance of power. Missiles in Cuba meant an advantage for the Soviets in their deadly arms race with the United States.

There was little debate on the part of the Kennedy team that the missiles, when ready, would be armed with nuclear warheads. Therefore, each missile the Soviets installed was fully capable of eradicating an American city. Given the range of the rockets, the entire eastern half of the United States—including the cities of New York and Washington, DC—could be hit by nuclear weapons launched from Cuba.

The United States, too, employed the strategy of putting IRBMs in allied countries near the enemy. At the time of the crisis, American IRBMs were in Great Britain, Italy, and Turkey, ready to be fired. The IRBMs carried nuclear

The Doomsday Map

A piece of Cuban Missile Crisis history was sold in Boston to the highest bidder in April 2018. The Doomsday Map, formerly a classified document, shows the locations of nine weapons installations in Cuba that United States forces may have targeted in the event of an attack. The map key summarizes locations of Soviet weapons to include MiG fighter jets and missiles.

President Kennedy gave the map that he referred to as a "victory map" to Defense Secretary Robert McNamara after the Cuban Missile Crisis. According to McNamara, "The President pored over this map before deciding to delay the attack." The information shown on the map was believed to be correct as of noon on October 27, 1962. The map, valued at $20,000.00, sold for $138,798.63.[2]

warheads and were aimed at targets somewhere in the Soviet Union. The missiles in Turkey were particularly upsetting to the Soviets. Turkey shared a common border with the Soviet Union. The missiles in Turkey were literally in the Soviet Union's backyard. The members of the Kennedy team were determined to do something to remove the Cuban missiles.

The team considered an air strike to "take out" the missiles with conventional bombs. According to historical documents, the debate went as follows:

President Kennedy: How effective can the take-out be, do they think?

General Maxwell Taylor: It'll never be a 100 percent, Mr. President, we know. We hope to take out the vast majority [of missiles] in the first strike, but this is not just one thing—one strike . . . but continuous air attack for whenever necessary . . . .

President Kennedy: Well, let's say we just take out the missile bases. Then they have some more there. Obviously they can get them in by submarine and so on.[3]

All team members gave their opinions. At the conclusion of the first-day's meeting, Kennedy ordered more U-2 flights. He also required absolute secrecy about the Cuban situation. At this point, the general public had no idea that the Soviets were building missile bases just 90 miles away from Florida. Nor did the Soviets know that the president and his staff were aware of their missile program.

Day Two: Wednesday, October 17, 1962

That morning, President Kennedy traveled to Connecticut to make a campaign speech for a fellow Democrat running for Congress. The speech had been on his schedule for months. The president wanted to abide by his schedule. To change his schedule would alert the country and the press that something urgent was happening in the world.

In Washington, the Kennedy team continued its high-stakes meetings. The team was now called ExComm, which stood for Executive Committee of the US National Security Council. The men examined new U-2 photos and found them frightening. Missiles were now visible. The fields being cleared for launch sites swarmed with Soviet and Cuban workers. Work was moving at a faster pace than originally thought. It appeared as if some of the missiles would be operational in a week or less. Robert Kennedy estimated that as many as eighty million Americans would be killed within minutes if a nuclear weapon was detonated.[4]

Never before had the Soviets stationed nuclear weapons beyond their borders. Also, in recent conferences with US officials, the Soviets claimed they were putting no offensive missiles in Cuba. The distinction between offensive and defensive weapons was critical. It was known that the Soviets were installing antiaircraft rockets in Cuba. Those rockets were designed to shoot down attacking aircraft and were considered defensive in nature. All countries had a right to defend their soil. However, there was nothing defensive about Soviet IRBMs with warheads aimed at the United States.

Khrushchev claimed he installed missiles in Cuba to protect that country from another American invasion. Thus, he was acting as a proper Communist, working to spread Communism to other lands. Khrushchev wrote: "If Cuba fell [to the capitalistic United States], other Latin American countries would reject us, claiming that for all our might the Soviet Union hadn't been able to do anything for Cuba except to make empty protests."[5]

By this time, Fidel Castro was an admitted Communist, and it was assumed that he, too, accepted the mission of expanding Communism. He hoped to encourage other Latin American governments to do so. He also wanted to prevent another American attack on his island nation.

Khrushchev was attracted to Communism as a young man because he believed the system gave working-class people a better life. Promising greater prosperity for the Soviet people, Khrushchev launched new farming and building projects. He portrayed himself as a factory worker with little refinement. Stocky and muscular looking, he used body language to express his moods. He shook with laughter when amused. When angry, he trembled, grew red faced, and shouted at opponents.

Members of ExComm knew Khrushchev's background and his personality. They also recognized him as a shrewd opponent. By putting missiles in Cuba, he certainly had other issues in mind rather than simply the expansion of Communism to the Americas. Perhaps he was pressuring the United States in order to win concessions in Berlin. American missiles in Turkey were an embarrassment as well as a threat to the Soviet Union. Maybe he thought the missiles on America's doorstep would give his rivals a taste of their own medicine.

Whatever Khrushchev's motives were, all ExComm men agreed the Cuban missiles must go. The team pondered two options: an air strike and a naval blockade. Both were acts of war and ultimately put the entire world at risk. Secretary of Defense Robert McNamara urged a blockade. Aerial bombing would kill many Cubans and Soviets. Such an attack would perhaps give Khrushchev no alternative but to strike back. A blockade meant surrounding Cuba with US naval ships. The American ships would intercept incoming vessels and prevent new missiles and crews from reaching the island. The blockade would do nothing about the missiles already in place. But McNamara hoped the blockade would not cost lives.

A Cloak of Secrecy

ExComm men were beginning to divide into "hawks" and "doves," although none of the team members used those terms. The hawks favored aggressive action against the missiles. Doves urged less drastic means. The doves suggested conferring with Khrushchev and trying to get him to remove the missiles peacefully.

The leading hawk was Air Force general Curtis LeMay. A stern, unsmiling man, LeMay now urged an immediate all-out air strike on the Cuban missiles. President Kennedy listened to LeMay's arguments for an air raid on Cuba. He asked how the Soviets were likely to respond to such an attack from the sky.

"They'll do nothing," said LeMay.

"Are you trying to tell me that they'll let us bomb their missiles, and kill a lot of [Soviets] and then do nothing?" Kennedy said. "If they don't do anything in Cuba, then they'll certainly do something in Berlin."[6]

Later, back in his office, Kennedy exclaimed, "Can you imagine LeMay saying a thing like that? If we listen to them [the hawkish generals], and do what they want us to do, none of us will be alive later to tell them that they were wrong."[7]

Day Three: Thursday, October 18, 1962

The most influential dove was Adlai Stevenson, America's ambassador to the United Nations. Stevenson was respected around the world for his intellectual approach to resolving disputes between nations. He believed that diplomacy and compromise, not force, should be employed to bring parties to agreement.

General Curtis LeMay was an advocate of nuclear weapons. During the Korean War, he wanted to drop nuclear bombs on major Korean cities to force an end to the war, but his superiors did not support this.

Stevenson favored setting up a conference between Kennedy and Khrushchev. The United States could offer to dismantle its missiles in Turkey in exchange for the USSR moving its weapons out of Cuba. At first, Kennedy rejected the missile trade-off suggestion. He thought it would look to the world as if the United States was backing down to Soviet pressure. However, the missiles in Turkey were more than five years old and were considered militarily obsolete. They were being replaced by newer rockets that could be

Democrat Adlai Stevenson (*right*) twice ran for the presidency (in 1952 and 1956) but lost each time. He also served as the governor of Illinois from 1948 to 1952.

fired with the push of a button without waiting for the fueling procedure.

At 9:00 p.m. the ExComm team moved from the State Department to the White House to confer with the president. These men were used to being ushered around Washington in private chauffeur-driven limousines. But too many such cars coming and going from the White House would arouse the suspicion of reporters. So nine men squeezed into one limousine for the quick trip to the White House. Robert Kennedy sat on another man's lap.[8]

The conference resumed at the president's office. The hawks gave their opinion. The doves provided their opinion. Day three ended with the consensus moving toward a blockade. It would start with US naval ships stopping Soviet vessels on the high seas. This was a militarily aggressive move, but, it was hoped, the blockade would force the Soviets to negotiate and let diplomacy resolve the crisis.

Despite the terrible tension surrounding ExComm members, day three closed on a note of humor. General Curtis LeMay told the president, "I say, you're in a pretty bad fix." Kennedy answered, "You're in [it] with me."[9] The men around them chuckled.

Day Four: Friday, October 19, 1962

President Kennedy flew to Ohio and later to Illinois. With congressional elections less than three weeks away, fellow Democrats were eager to have the president speak on their behalf. Making these routine campaign appearances was important in order to keep the Cuban situation secret. But newspaper reporters began to notice events behind the scenes. Army and Marine units were on alert in Florida in case an invasion of Cuba was ordered. Several

Florida newspapers had already reported on the increase of military truck columns on the state's highways.

Kennedy gave the appearance that everything was fine in the nation. The president was forty-five years old in 1962, youthful compared to recent presidents. He also had movie-star good looks. His beautiful wife and adorable kids were darlings in the eyes of the public. Kennedy was a great campaigner, greeting the masses and shaking hands while flashing his famous smile. But as he spoke to the excited crowds in October 1962, his thoughts were probably on Cuba and the Soviet missiles there.

Operation Blue Moon

Operation Blue Moon was a top-secret mission dispatched on October 19, 1962, by the United States during the Cuban Missile Crisis. According to previously top-secret documents, the objective of the operation was "low altitude photographic reconnaissance of selected military and intelligence targets on the Island of Cuba." To accomplish the objective, F8U aircraft would be utilized. The rationale for Operation Blue Moon was "to prevent the secret accumulation in the island of arms that can be used for offensive purposes."[10]

CIA documents declassified in March 2004 indicate that should an incident happen over Cuba, a hostile territory, the pilot was under orders to destroy his aircraft at sea. If he was captured, he could only provide his name, rank, and serial number.

In Washington, ExComm met all day Friday and into Friday night. The ExComm men took a vote and the majority recommended a blockade of Cuba. This was simply a recommendation. The final decision was to be made by President Kennedy.

6

THE ABYSS OF
DESTRUCTION

On the morning of October 20, 1962, President Kennedy learned from his brother that work on the missiles and the launch sites in Cuba was proceeding more rapidly than anticipated. Robert Kennedy also alerted his brother that the press was becoming increasingly more suspicious of a crisis of some sort. He suggested that perhaps someone on the White House staff was leaking information.

The phone call from Robert Kennedy put the president in a dilemma. He was currently in Chicago and due to fly to California that afternoon, but he knew that he needed to be back in Washington, DC, to address the continuing crisis. However, he was not ready to alert the nation. In order to conceal the true reason for the president's cancellation of the California engagement, it was announced that President Kennedy had a cold and needed rest. Therefore, he would be returning to the capital.

Kennedy was seen leaving his downtown Chicago hotel and getting into a limousine for the ride to the airport. He was wearing a hat, which was unusual for him. On this day, though, he wore one because he wanted people to think he had a cold.

Help from Mother Nature

In order to return to the White House as the Cuban Missile Crisis escalated, President Kennedy used the excuse that he had a cold. However, how is it possible to hide from prying eyes movement of a fleet of ships? Thankfully, Mother Nature provided an excuse with Hurricane Ella. Officials used the formation of the hurricane as the excuse to explain the movement of the fleet toward Cuba.

Hurricane Ella began to develop in the southeastern Bahamas on October 14, 1962. By the next day, it was officially a tropical storm. The storm reached hurricane strength on October 17. A ship 90 miles (145 km) southeast of the center of the hurricane reported seas of up to 45 feet (14 m) on the 18th.

Hurricane Ella lasted until October 23. While property damage was minor, two fishermen who set out from Charleston, South Carolina, lost their lives in the hurricane during its closest approach to the Atlantic coast. They were never found.

A Strict Quarantine

Upon arriving in Washington, the president received distressing news. Intelligence reports claimed that as many as eight Soviet missiles were already operational.[1] Other missiles were being made ready at a rapid pace.

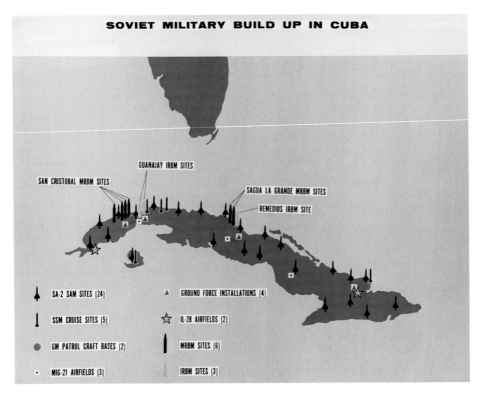

A map of Cuba from about 1962 shows the number and type of installation at each Soviet missile site.

No one knows Kennedy's inner thoughts as he faced this crisis. The coming clash loomed as a duel between Soviet premier Khrushchev and him. At this point, Fidel Castro was seen as a minor player. The president and his staff believed that Khrushchev had the final authority to fire the Cuban missiles and plunge the world into nuclear war.

During the Cuban Missile Crisis, Kennedy often told the ExComm team that he did not want to put Khrushchev in a corner. He hoped to give the Soviet premier room to maneuver so he could ease his way out of this difficult situation. To act harshly at first, such as launching a surprise air raid on the missile sites, might force Khrushchev to strike back with harshness of his own. Khrushchev could move troops into Berlin. He could bomb the American missile bases in Turkey. Also, some of the missiles in Cuba would probably survive an American air strike. Those remaining missiles could then be fired on US cities with great loss of life.

Day Five: Saturday, October 20, 1962

Robert Kennedy claimed the president made his final decision on Saturday afternoon, day five of the crisis.[2] He determined the United States would blockade Cuba to prevent Soviet ships from bringing more missiles to the island. The blockade was not to be called a blockade, however, because that word could be interpreted as an act of war. Instead, the navy would "quarantine" Cuba.

In 1962, a naval destroyer, the USS *Vesole*, intercepts the Soviet ship *Potzunov* as it leaves Cuba carrying missiles. *Vesole* patrolled the area between Key West, Florida, and Havana, Cuba.

This meant that the navy would only prevent offensive weapons from entering Cuba. Ships would be stopped at sea, inspected, and allowed to pass if they contained only commercial cargo.

The quarantine policy left many issues and questions unresolved. What if ships refused to stop when challenged? What about the missiles already in place on Cuba? What of Berlin, Turkey, and all the other locations where the United States was vulnerable to Soviet attack? Dangerous possibilities abounded. But the blockade—called a quarantine—was ordered.

Day Six: Sunday, October 21, 1962

It was a brilliant fall day in Washington, DC. Golden sunlight shown on the National Mall, the Capitol building, and the statues and monuments. On this Sunday afternoon, people around the country watched television shows such as *Lassie, Father Knows Best,* and *Bonanza.* Unemployment was relatively low. Businesses thrived. People generally had a positive outlook about their lives and the future of their children. But while tourists in the capital enjoyed this fine fall day, the tension inside the White House reached almost unbearable levels.

President Kennedy wrote letters outlining his plans to allies in Europe, Latin America, and Asia. Letters went out to American embassies around the world warning of the possibility of demonstrations and riots. Finally, a letter went to the Kremlin, the seat of Soviet government in Moscow. Kennedy intended to make a speech to the nation the next day. The speech would announce the quarantine plans. Proper diplomacy required him to inform his adversaries of his actions before the national address. Kennedy did not want the Soviet premier to learn of American intentions with the rest of the world through watching it on television.

All branches of the armed forces were made ready. Ships went to sea to form a ring around Cuba. Troops relocated to Florida and other southern states in case events called for an invasion of the island.

President Executive Order 13526

In 1991, Robert Gates, director of the CIA, recommended that the agency begin declassifying government documents. The CIA Task Force on Openness was formed along with the CIA Historical Review Board. The first classified documents related to the Cuban Missile Crisis were released in the fall of 1992.

In 1995, the Historical Review Board was replaced with a more formal group, the Historical Review Panel (HRP). The HRP advises the CIA on declassification issues and protects intelligence sources and methods. The panel also assists in developing subjects of historical and scholarly interest for declassification review.

Since 2009, the HRP has operated in accordance to the President Executive Order 13526. This order outlines the system to be used for classifying, safeguarding, and declassifying national security information. The panel must balance the free flow of information from the government to the American people while also protecting the country's security.

Reporters observed these massive troop movements and guessed the source of the tension was Cuba. The *Washington Post* ran the headline: "Marine Moves in South Linked to Cuban Crisis."[3] The *New York Herald Tribune* said: "Top-Secret Doings in Capital; A Cuban-Berlin Strategy Step?"[4] President Kennedy suspected that someone on his team was leaking information to reporters. "This town is a sieve," he complained.[5]

A Public Announcement on Day Seven: Monday, October 22, 1962

The White House announced the president would address the nation later that night at 7 p.m. on a matter of grave importance. Before the speech, Kennedy met with key members of Congress to brief them about the missiles in Cuba and his plan for the quarantine. One of the senators was Hubert Humphrey of Minnesota. Humphrey had run for president in the Democratic primary elections of 1960 and was defeated by Kennedy. At the end of the briefing, Humphrey was heard to say, "Thank God I am not the President of the United States."[6]

Diplomatic teams got ready. Ambassador Adlai Stevenson prepared to take America's case before the United Nations (UN). The Organization of American States (OAS) would also be called upon to lend its diplomatic efforts to a peaceful resolution of the crisis. The OAS was an association of Latin American countries.

That evening all regular television programs were canceled so the presidential speech could air. Millions of Americans watched as their president's face appeared on their TV screens. Kennedy looked grim as he revealed to the world that the Soviet Union had placed offensive weapons on the island of Cuba and that the only possible purpose

John F. Kennedy actually had two speeches drafted for the October 22, 1962 televised address: one to announce the naval quarantine and another to announce an actual air attack on Cuba. Fortunately, the latter was not needed.

of the weapons was to establish nuclear strike capability against the United States and other nations in the Western Hemisphere.

The president then outlined the steps that the United States would implement in response including the naval quarantine. He made it clear that if the USSR continued efforts to make the missiles operational, then the United States was prepared to take additional actions. President Kennedy also warned that any missile launch from Cuba would be viewed as an attack by the Soviet Union. He urged Khrushchev to immediately remove the missiles from Cuba.

President Kennedy concluded the speech on a somber note: "The path we have chosen for the present is full of hazards, as all paths are. . . . The cost of freedom is always high—and Americans have always paid it. . . . Our goal is not the victory of might . . . not peace at the expense of freedom, but both peace and freedom, here in this hemisphere, and, we hope, around the world. God willing, that goal will be achieved."[7]

CONTINUED AND INCREASED CLOSE SURVEILLANCE OF CUBA

Throughout the Cuban Missile Crisis, ExComm often worked long hours. Meals were rushed or missed entirely. There were even nights when committee members did not return home. Instead, they remained in their offices as they awaited the next reports. Following the president's address, Secretary of State Dean Rusk and Undersecretary George Ball never made it home to their own beds. Instead, they spent the night in their offices, sleeping on sofas. Upon waking up on the morning of October 23, Rusk said to Ball, "Good morning. We have won a considerable victory. You and I are still alive."[1]

Far at sea, Soviet ships steamed toward Cuba. Awaiting them were US warships. The light and fast destroyers were to play a prime role in this operation. The plan was for destroyers to approach the Soviet ships, order them to stop, and inspect them. One Russian-speaking officer was placed on each American ship. If the Soviet vessels refused to stop, the destroyers would fire a warning shot with their guns. If they still failed to halt, the destroyer captains were ordered to fire at their rudders or propellers to disable the ships.[2]

Such confrontations on the high seas were fraught with danger. It was known that Soviet submarines were patrolling the waters off Cuba. The subs were quite capable of sinking an American ship. Neither Khrushchev nor Kennedy wanted war, but events could easily spiral out of control. One confrontational ship commander on either side could do something foolish and escalate matters quickly. In a nightmare scenario, neither Kennedy nor Khrushchev could halt the escalation of violence.

Cuba was virtually under an umbrella of American aircraft. Two of the ships on blockade duty were large aircraft carriers, the *Independence* and the *Enterprise.* Each carrier housed upward of a hundred aircraft. Aircraft flew a daily average of one hundred twenty flights from the *Enterprise* during the crisis. Land-based planes joined the naval aircraft. A total of about five hundred fifty fighters and bombers were set to attack Cuba if an air strike were called.[3] Army troops and Marines were gathering at southern ports in preparation for an invasion. All military leaves were canceled.

An Active Threat

Fear and tension swept the United States. World War II and the Korean War were still recent memories, but those conflicts were fought on faraway battlefronts. Now, the American people faced an impending war where deadly missiles were only a short distance away. Suddenly there was a very real danger of unseen warheads plunging from the sky. Entire cities might disappear under the great mushroom-shaped clouds that follow an atomic blast.

The USS *Enterprise* was the world's first nuclear-powered aircraft carrier. It was 1,101 feet (336 m) in length and 252 feet (77 m) wide at its widest point and carried a crew of 4,600.

Throughout the crisis, workers reported to their jobs, and students went to school. However, fear was evident. A Columbia University professor who knew President Kennedy wrote him: "The reaction among students here . . . was qualitatively different from anything I've ever witnessed before. . . . These kids were literally scared for their lives and were astonished, somehow, that their lives could be risked by an American initiative."[4]

Day Eight: Tuesday, October 23, 1962

At 9:00 a.m., the Organization of American States (OAS) met in an emergency session. In the midst of the crisis, all Western Hemisphere countries felt threatened by nuclear weapons. The OAS voted overwhelmingly to condemn the Soviet missiles based in Cuba.

At noon, Kennedy received a cabled letter from Moscow. It was the first official Soviet reaction to the quarantine. The letter denounced the quarantine as a violation of international law. Several members of the Kennedy team pointed out that the quarantine was consistent with the Monroe Doctrine. However, the president did not want to invoke the principles of the Monroe Doctrine. In the past, the Monroe Doctrine had been used as an excuse to invade Latin American nations. Kennedy wanted Latin American unity as he pressured the Soviets to withdraw from Cuba. The OAS vote affirmed he had achieved that unity.

The last line of the Khrushchev letter to Kennedy was significant. The Soviet chief offered to meet with the American president and discuss a peaceful solution. However, he warned, "If the United States insists on war [then] we'll all meet in hell."[5]

Day Nine: Wednesday, October 24, 1962

There always loomed the fear that one miscalculation, one wrong move, could plunge the world into war. President Kennedy labored to keep the situation under his control, but was that possible? He and his team sat in offices in the White House. Hundreds of miles away, on the high seas, ships were about to confront other ships. No one in the White House was able to supervise or regulate events about to take place on the ocean. Accidental war haunted the minds of those involved in the crisis.

The Gold Codes

In order for the president to authorize a nuclear attack, he must use nuclear codes. These codes, known as Gold Codes, are written on a plastic card known as "the biscuit." The president keeps this card in his possession.

Once the president orders an attack, the Pentagon confirms the codes. The order is then carried throughout the chain of command. This includes bombers, submarines, and missiles that make up the unit referred to as the nuclear triad.

A two-man rule exists at each step so that no single person is ever responsible for launching a nuclear strike. The first bombs would strike the intended target within thirty minutes. The Secretary of Defense is legally required to comply with the president's order. A strike can be stopped only if multiple people in the chain of command disobey the order.

Stores around the country reported a rush of customers buying canned goods. Canned food could serve as emergency rations in the event of an air raid. Police stations were flooded with calls: Where is the city's air-raid shelter? How much warning will we get? Are the Soviets going to invade? Will they bomb us?

Fear was especially prevalent in Florida and the southeastern states. Long military truck columns rumbled over highways in the South, adding to the urgent sense of war. The trucks towed artillery pieces and tanks on flatbed trailers. Hotels in the southeast experienced a rash of cancellations. Vacationers from the cold states up north decided to stay home this winter. With war pending, a vacation in the sun was simply not worth the risk.

Tensions on Both Sides

At ten in the morning, Secretary of Defense McNamara made an important announcement to the ExComm meeting. Radio reports said the American fleet was about to make its first interception. Two Soviet ships were just a few miles away from American destroyers. The ships were in radio contact with Moscow. The ExComm men believed the Soviet vessels were under direct orders from the Kremlin. Would the enemy ships stop when commanded or would they defy the quarantine?

Adding to the tension, Secretary McNamara learned a Soviet submarine patrolled the waters near the two merchant ships.

"Isn't there some way we can avoid having our first exchange with a [Soviet] submarine—almost anything but that," said President Kennedy.

Grocery store workers try to figure out where to place large orders as scared people rush to buy supplies. President Kennedy encouraged Americans to be prepared for a nuclear attack and advocated for fallout shelters. During the crisis, many Americans heeded his advice and stocked shelters with canned food, water, battery-powered radios, and first-aid kits.

Robert McNamara was the country's eighth Secretary of Defense and served under John F. Kennedy and Lyndon B. Johnson. Prior to this, he was a commissioned army officer.

Nuclear Responsibilities

The Department of Defense (DOD) and the Department of Energy (DOE) share responsibility of the nuclear weapons in the United States. The DOD develops, deploys, and operates the missiles as well as the aircraft that deliver them. The DOE works with the National Nuclear Security Administration to oversee research, development, and testing. The nuclear weapons complex, referred to as the Nuclear Security Enterprise, consists primarily of nine sites in seven states. There is also a Tennessee Valley Authority nuclear reactor that produces tritium for nuclear weapons.

Five of the facilities produce and assemble components for nuclear weapons. Two other sites dismantle retired weapons. Another location maintains the ability to resume nuclear explosive testing if ordered to do so by the president. An additional site manages plutonium-contaminated waste produced by nuclear weapons facilities.

"No," answered McNamara, "there's too much danger to our ships. There is no alternative."[6]

At 10:25 a messenger who handed a letter to John McCone, a member of ExComm, interrupted the meeting. "Mr. President," McCone said, "we have a preliminary report which seems to indicate that some of the [Soviet] ships have stopped dead in the water."[7]

A hush that lasted several minutes overcame the meeting. Robert Kennedy checked the clock. It was 10:32 a.m.

John McCone broke the silence. "The report is accurate, Mr. President," said McCone. "Six ships previously on their way to Cuba at the edge of the quarantine line have stopped or have turned back toward the Soviet Union."[8]

President Kennedy then told his naval aide to radio all American warships. They were not to pursue the retreating Soviet vessels. As a navy veteran who had been in combat, the president knew about armed clashes at sea. He wanted to avoid any kind of a sea battle at this point. He insisted US warships give the Soviets plenty of room to return home.

Secretary of State Dean Rusk then made a remark to fellow members of ExComm. The secretary compared the United States and USSR standoff to a fight between two schoolboys. He said, "We are eyeball to eyeball, and I think the other fellow just blinked."[9]

The immediate crisis of a confrontation at sea had been averted. The relief felt by all ExComm members was overwhelming. The first direct confrontation between the two nuclear superpowers had ended and the other fellow had blinked.

8

PATIENCE AND WILL ARE TESTED

By October 25, the US military was preparing for war. Though most of the Soviet vessels in route to Cuba had stopped or turned around, dozens of missiles were on Cuban soil already. A potentially deadly confrontation was still possible.

The Strategic Air Command (SAC) raised its alert status to DEFCON-2, one step away from war. Never before in the long history of the Cold War did the alert status reach the level of DEFCON-2.[1] The advanced DEFCON alert meant that nuclear bombs were loaded onto giant SAC bombers and made ready for use at a moment's notice.[2] American crews manning ballistic missiles armed with nuclear warheads also went on high alert.

Commander in Chief, Strategic Air Command General Thomas Power ordered forces to DEFCON 2 at 10:00 a.m. on October 24, 1962. During the crisis and immediately following the thirteen days, 2,088 B-52 aircraft were launched.

Fear tightened its grip on the American people. Highways in Florida swarmed with military traffic. Miami telephone companies claimed long-distance calls were up

A Boeing B-52 Stratofortress bomber carries two missiles.

25 percent.[3] Officials in the New York City school system ordered air-raid drills.

At sea, a few Soviet ships continued to advance toward Cuba. American destroyers closed in on those vessels. The first actual intercept of a Soviet cargo craft took place on October 25, 1962. At 8:00 a.m., the American destroyer *Gearing* approached the Soviet tanker *Bucharest* and ordered it to stop. Over the radio, the tanker captain said his ship carried only petroleum products. The exchange between the two ships was radioed to the ExComm team in Washington where decisions on enforcing the quarantine were being made. Kennedy's men decided to let the *Bucharest* go without boarding the vessel. It was unlikely a tanker would carry missiles.

Alert Condition

In 1957, the Air Force created the North American Aerospace Defense Command (NORAD) to provide early warning and defense against nuclear threats. NORAD proposed the Defense Condition (DEFCON) system in 1959. It is used in the event of a national emergency.

The system is a series of seven different alert conditions (LERTCONs). The seven LERTCONs are broken down into five DEFCONs and two emergency conditions (EMERGCONs). DEFCONs are used by the Joint Chiefs of Staff and the commanders of the unified commands to describe the state of readiness of the country's military forces. DEFCON 5 represents normal peacetime readiness. DEFCON 1 indicates maximum force readiness.

EMERGCONs are national level reactions in response to missile attacks. A Defense Emergency indicates a major attack upon United States forces overseas or on allied forces in any area. An Air Defense Emergency indicates that an attack on the continental United States is considered probable, imminent, or is taking place.

This first intercept, though it was uneventful, triggered a debate among the ExComm members. Some believed the quarantine ought to be stepped up and apply to all goods heading toward Cuba. Why not cut off their supplies? A shortage of any product, such as petroleum to fuel trucks, could slow the Soviet technicians. The arguments raged at ExComm meetings, but the scope of the quarantine was never expanded.

Clearly Offensive Weapons Revealed on Day Ten: Thursday, October 25, 1962

The drama on the tenth day of the crisis shifted to New York City and the United Nations (UN). An emergency UN session was called to discuss a peaceful solution to the crisis. Providing a format for debate was a major function of the world body. On the floor of the UN, adversary nations could battle with words instead of weapons. Millions watched this UN debate on television, including President Kennedy

Adlai Stevenson, the American ambassador, stood before the assembly of nations. Stevenson was an elegant speaker and known to be a mild-mannered and gentlemanly individual. He faced Ambassador Valerian Zorin, the Soviet delegate. Zorin had claimed repeatedly that there were no Soviet offensive missiles in Cuba.

"Do you, Ambassador Zorin," Stevenson said, "deny that the USSR has placed and is placing medium and intermediate-range ballistic missiles and sites in Cuba?"

Zorin hesitated as if waiting to hear the translation over his earphones. Yet he spoke English well, and Stevenson thought he was simply stalling.

"Yes or no," snapped Stevenson, "don't wait for the translation—yes or no?"

Zorin said, "I am not in an American courtroom, sir, and therefore I do not wish to answer. . . ."

Stevenson interrupted him, "You are in the courtroom of world opinion right now, and you can answer yes or no."

"You will have your answer in due course," said Ambassador Zorin.

"I am prepared to wait for my answer until hell freezes over," said Stevenson.[4]

Ambassador Stevenson then motioned to an aide. A large photo propped up on an easel was brought before the assembly. It was a picture taken from an American reconnaissance plane. It clearly showed a Soviet missile site. Presenting this reconnaissance photo was a dramatic move on Stevenson's part. Before the entire world, Stevenson exposed Zorin as a liar.

At the October 25 televised UN gathering, Adlai Stevenson confronted his Soviet counterpart, Valerian Zorin, about the Cuban missile sites. Aerial photos of Soviet missile bases in Cuba were displayed for all the delegates to view for themselves.

Tensions Are Removed on Day Eleven: Friday, October 26, 1962

Early in the morning, another ship heading for Cuba was stopped by American destroyers. It was the *Marucla*, a Lebanese freighter manned by a Greek crew and leased by the USSR. One of the destroyers stopping the vessel was the DD850, the *Joseph P. Kennedy Jr.*, a destroyer named after President Kennedy's older brother who was killed in World War II. A team of American sailors boarded the *Marucla* to inspect its cargo.

One American officer spoke Russian, but the captain of the *Marucla* was Greek. None of the Americans spoke the Greek language, so the men communicated using hand gestures. The captain served the Americans coffee while they looked around. They found nothing suspicious and left the ship. This event was largely a demonstration. ExComm members doubted that the Soviets would put offensive weapons on a foreign flagship. However, the Kennedy team wanted to prove to the Soviet leaders that the US Navy could and would board one of their vessels.[5]

October 26 marked the fourth day after the Kennedy speech that announced the presence of Soviet missiles on Cuban soil. The newscaster Chet Huntley called that presidential address "the toughest and the most grim speech by a president since December 7, 1941, when President Roosevelt spoke to the Congress and the nation about the day of infamy . . . the attack on Pearl Harbor."[6]

One of the newsmen keeping the country informed was John Scali of ABC television. He covered the State Department and had friends in that agency. The tense international situation was keeping him as well as all the other newscasters busy. Instead of taking a leisurely lunch on October 26, Scali ate a bologna sandwich at his

John Scali's service to his country did not end with the Cuban Missile Crisis. He was the US Ambassador to the UN from 1973 to 1975.

desk. Suddenly, his phone rang. It was Aleksandr Fomin, the official public-affairs officer for the Soviet Embassy. It is unclear exactly why the Soviets approached Scali at this time instead of someone closer to President Kennedy, but this first contact ultimately produced a diplomatic breakthrough. Fomin suggested that he and Scali meet for lunch right away. Scali knew that Fomin was not his real name and that his work in public affairs was a cover-up. His real name was Alexander Feklisov, and he was a Soviet spy.[7]

At lunch, Fomin told Scali the situation was very serious and that "war seems about to break out."[8] He asked if the United States would be receptive to a deal. The USSR would withdraw its missiles in exchange for a US pledge not to invade Cuba. Scali said he did not know if American leaders would approve of such a deal. However, he knew Fomin was a high Soviet official, and he reasoned that this proposal would have to come from top leaders in Moscow. Scali contacted his friends in the State Department.

From the beginning of the crisis, Kennedy and Khrushchev had been exchanging letters, which came as cablegrams (long-distance telegrams that transmitted messages). Many of Khrushchev's cablegrams tended to ramble, but he repeatedly said that nuclear war was madness. Like Kennedy, he expressed the fear that war could break out despite the efforts of the two leaders to stop it. In one letter, he said: "[We] ought not now to pull on the ends of the rope in which you have tied the knot of war, because the more the two of us pull, the tighter that knot will be tied. And the moment may come when that knot will be tied so tight that even he who tied it will not have the strength to untie it."[9]

Was Nuclear War Closer Than Anyone Thought?

Beginning in 1987, a series of five meetings were held at various sites to discuss the implications of the Cuban Missile Crisis. The meetings brought together scholars and key officials who played an active role during the Cuban Missile Crisis. Representatives such as former US Secretary of Defense Robert McNamara and Aleksandr Alekseev, who had served as the Soviet ambassador to Cuba, participated. Fidel Castro also participated in the January 1992 meeting, which convened in Havana.

The meetings provided insight never before revealed or understood. Perhaps most eye opening was the realization that Castro was committed to fight even if that meant war. Though a nuclear war would mean almost certain annihilation of Cuba, his revolutionary mindset was that his country would not be viewed as cowardly. It would go down fighting in defense of Cuba. Castro also confirmed that he was completely left out of the negotiations between Kennedy and Khrushchev.

Yet none of Khrushchev's letters or cablegrams contained an idea or a specific plan suggesting how to defuse the dangerous nuclear standoff. The proposal by Fomin to Scali may have been the initial steps to a plan.

At 6:00 in the evening (1:00 a.m. Moscow time), a letter arrived from Khrushchev via teletype. For the first time, Khrushchev admitted he had placed offensive missiles in Cuba. He also repeated the Fomin plan. "This is my proposal," the Soviet leader said. "No more weapons to Cuba and those within Cuba withdrawn or destroyed, and you reciprocate by withdrawing your blockade and also agree not to invade Cuba."[10] The letter was perhaps a vital first step in peacefully resolving the crisis.

The Soviets had not told Castro or other Cuban leaders about their offer to Kennedy, though. At this stage in the crisis, the proposals and counterproposals were exchanged only between the two superpowers. The fate of Cuba was a minor consideration when weighed against the possibility of World War III.

Meanwhile, the United States remained in a state of high anxiety. The missile crisis was on everyone's mind, and it dominated conversations between friends and neighbors. Americans were nervous, on edge, and fearful. In Jacksonville, Florida, an air-raid siren accidentally sounded, and the city's police department was flooded with forty thousand phone calls.[11]

FORCE SHALL NOT BE USED

On October 27, a Soviet submarine, B-59, was submerged off the coast of Cuba. The submarine was armed with nuclear weapons. Because the submarine had been submerged so long, it was running short of energy and fresh air. The temperature inside the submarine was stifling.

On the surface, eleven American destroyers and an aircraft carrier surrounded B-59. In order to force the submarine to surface, the Americans were dropping Practice Depth Chargers (PDCs). While depth chargers are typically explosive, the PDCs were signaling devices only. However, those aboard the Soviet submarine did not know that the PDCs were not real depth chargers. Because their communication devices were damaged and contact with Moscow was not possible, the crew aboard B-59 thought that the war had started. They believed that the Americans were attacking their submarine.

Some crew members wanted to launch a nuclear torpedo. The submarine commander, Captain Valentin Savitski, screamed at fellow officers, "We're going to blast them now! We will die, but we will sink them all—we will not disgrace our Navy."[1] However, Captain Vasili Arkhipov refused to give the order. He finally managed to calm Captain Savitski and brought the submarine to the surface. After recharging its batteries, B-59 limped toward home. It was exactly the type of incident that both Kennedy and Khrushchev feared most. One volatile commander came close to touching off a wave of events that could have snowballed into nuclear war.

Patience and Restraint Shown on Day Twelve: Saturday, October 27, 1962

Major Rudolf Anderson from Greenville, South Carolina, was a U-2 pilot. He had already completed five missions over Cuba and was not scheduled to fly on October 27. However, when he was told to go up, he was prepared to do so. He left McCoy Air Force Base in Florida just after 9 a.m. The skies were fairly clear with a mix of sun and clouds. He flew at 72,000 feet (21,946 m) well aware of the importance of the mission and the photographs he captured.[2]

On the ground in Cuba, Soviet radar was tracking the U-2's flight. For nearly an hour, they watched as the target referred to as Target 33 circled the island. Just after 11:00 a.m., a decision was made to destroy the target. At 11:19, two surface-to-air missiles were fired at Major Anderson's U-2. Though the missiles did not make a direct hit, pieces of shrapnel, which are remnants of an explosive device, pierced the plane and Major Anderson. The damaged U-2 plunged down to Earth and crashed. Major Rudolf Anderson was killed.[3]

The news was greeted with shock and gloom by the ExComm team. Everyone felt sorry for Anderson and his family, but this also meant the Soviet surface-to-air missiles

(SAMs) were operational. President Kennedy said, "How can we send any more U-2 pilots into this area tomorrow unless we take out all of the SAM sites? We are now in an entirely new ball game."[4]

President Kennedy later sent a letter to Major Anderson's wife. He included a handwritten statement, "Your husband's mission was of the greatest importance, but I know how deeply you must feel his loss."[5]

The death of Major Anderson dashed the hopeful mood that prevailed with the Kennedy team after the Scali and Fomin exchange and the Khrushchev letter. They also

Major Anderson's military funeral took place November 1, 1962. Following his death, Major Anderson received a number of posthumous honors including the first-ever Air Force Cross, which is the service's highest award. He was the only U-2 pilot who flew during the crisis to receive the award.

A Truth Revealed

For years following the crisis, there was misunderstanding regarding who ordered the shoot-down of Major Anderson's plane. Did the order to fire come from Khrushchev? Did Fidel Castro literally push the button and fire on the U-2? At the Havana Conference in January 1992, what actually transpired on October 27, 1962, was finally revealed.

General Anatoly Gribkov, who helped plan the secret deployment of the missiles to Cuba in 1962, stated that Major Anderson was shot down with a Soviet missile under Soviet command based in Cuba. General Stephan Grechko issued the order. There were no orders from Moscow nor was Fidel Castro responsible. Castro did, however, believe that a surprise air attack was imminent, and he supported taking whatever steps were necessary to protect Cuba. When Khrushchev was informed of the shoot-down, he was very disturbed and concerned that the Unites States would view the act as an escalation by the Soviets.

learned that personnel in the Soviet Embassy in Washington were destroying all their sensitive records.[6] Such destruction of paper records was often a final step before war. Once more, the world seemed to be at the brink of destruction.

Adding to the atmosphere of despair was a second letter from Khrushchev. This letter was broadcast by radio to the Soviet people. It brought a new demand to the table. The United States must agree to withdraw its missiles from Turkey before the Soviet Union dismantled its weapons in Cuba.

The demand for a missile trade-off presented the Kennedy team with a dilemma. The missiles in Turkey were obsolete. Plans had already been made to remove them from Turkish soil. But could the United States take them away now in the face of Soviet pressure? ExComm feared such a move would give the appearance of weakness. On the one hand, it seemed senseless to risk war over a few obsolete missiles based in Turkey. However, friends and allies around the world could lose respect for the United States if it appeared to concede to Soviet demands.

On all fronts, the situation worsened by the hour. Reports from Cuba said the Soviets were working day and night to get all the missiles operational. Top American generals recommended the United States launch an air strike on Monday, followed by an invasion. Robert Kennedy stated later that day twelve would prove to be one of the most trying and difficult days of the Cuban Missile Crisis.[7]

Finally, the ExComm men decided on a response to Khrushchev's letter. Robert Kennedy suggested to the president that he simply ignore the demands in the latest letter and respond instead to the initial letter.[8] President Kennedy agreed with his brother and wrote a letter that agreed to the earlier proposal. The United States pledged not to invade Cuba in exchange for a Soviet withdrawal of its missiles. The Cuba–Turkey trade-off was simply ignored. The letter was sent by cable. Everyone waited for the Soviet leaders' reaction.

Moving the World Back from the Brink on Day Thirteen: Sunday, October 28, 1962

On this Sunday morning, church attendance was up by 20 percent across the country.[9] In New York, the largest peace demonstration ever seen in that city assembled in front of the UN building. People prayed for peace.

During the Cuban Missile Crisis, there were peace marches across the United States. In Boston, Cuban refugees marched to show their support for President Kennedy.

The military prepared for war. The alert status for the Strategic Air Command remained at DEFCON-2. Planes were readied to bomb Cuba in twenty-four hours. Five million pamphlets were printed up warning Cuban civilians to take cover.[10] The pamphlets were to be dropped before the actual bombs were released. Soldiers and Marines were massed along the Florida coast, armed for invasion. More

than one hundred naval vessels crowded the coastal waters in anticipation of a landing on Cuban beaches.[11] These vast forces were poised to spring into action at the command of one man—President John F. Kennedy.

That morning, Kennedy dressed to go to church. The radio in his bedroom played popular music. The music stopped abruptly as an announcer told listeners to stand by for an important news bulletin. Kennedy was the most powerful man in the world. Yet that morning, he heard the news like anyone else—over the radio. At 9:00 a.m. Washington time (6:00 p.m. Moscow time), a spokesman in Moscow broadcast a new letter from Khrushchev to Kennedy: "In order to complete with greater speed the liquidation of the conflict dangerous to the cause of peace . . . [I have] issued a new order on the dismantling of the weapons which you describe as 'offensive,' and their crating and return to the Soviet Union."[12]

Khrushchev said he would immediately remove Soviet missiles in exchange for a US pledge not to invade Cuba. The ploy had worked. In his letter, Kennedy avoided the sticky problems associated with a Cuba–Turkey missile trade by simply not mentioning it. This letter from Khrushchev did not mention the trade either.

To the relief of the entire world, the Cuban Missile Crisis was over. On that Sunday morning, men and women around the globe celebrated peace and freedom from fear.

Only a handful of people were aware of a silent agreement made between the United States and the USSR. The night before day thirteen, Robert Kennedy had met with Soviet Ambassador Anatoly Dobrynin in Washington. At the meeting, Robert Kennedy said the US missiles in Turkey and Italy would soon be removed as a matter of course.

An informal deal was struck. The United States would remove its missiles from the Soviet Union's doorstep, but the removal would not be considered a trade for those in Cuba. The missiles in Turkey and Italy would simply be retired. Robert Kennedy was careful to put nothing in writing. He simply gave his word that the Turkish missiles would soon be gone. In April 1963, they were withdrawn from Turkey and Italy.

On the evening of day thirteen, President Kennedy watched the televised news program, *Washington Report,* which was broadcast live over CBS. Sitting at his side was Press Secretary Pierre Salinger. Reports from Cuba claimed

Anatoly Dobrynin served as the Soviet ambassador to Washington from 1962 until 1986 and was instrumental during the crisis, secretly meeting with Robert Kennedy three times in October 1962.

The Missile Defense Agency

The Missile Defense Agency (MDA) is an agency within the Department of Defense. It develops, tests, and fields a ballistic missile defense system to defend the United States, its deployed forces, and its allies. The agency dates back to 1983 when President Ronald Reagan launched the Strategic Defense Initiative.

The MDA focuses its efforts to stay ahead of foreign nuclear threats. Antimissile technologies being pursued include airborne lasers capable of stopping enemy missiles in the early stages of flight. The agency is also investigating ways to counter a missile attack before a launch through strategies that involve cyber-attacks and electronic warfare. Also in development is greater missile defense capability in space with a space-based missile defense layer.

Soviet technicians had already started disassembling the missiles. On the television news show, two newsmen hailed the ending of the Cuban Missile Crisis as a victory for the United States. Referring to an American victory and Soviet defeat concerned Kennedy. He feared that such talk might anger Khrushchev and cause him to change his mind. The president asked Salinger to contact the news station and have them refrain from such statements. The newsmen did as Salinger advised.[13]

PEACE AND SECURITY FOR ALL

While many in the world breathed a sigh of relief following the peaceful resolution to the Cuban Missile Crisis, Fidel Castro was fuming. He did not play a role in the negotiations between the United States and the USSR, and this angered him. The revolutionary leader was fully prepared to fight to the death. Though the outcome prevented a US invasion of Cuba, it did nothing to prevent a revolt against his government by anti-Communist Cubans. Fidel Castro wrote Khrushchev: "Countless eyes of Cuban and Soviet men who were willing to die with supreme dignity shed tears upon learning about the surprising, sudden and practically unconditional decision to withdraw the weapons."[1]

Castro did impose his own partial will on the settlement to the event called the October Crisis in Cuba. The Soviet Union had agreed to allow UN inspectors to come to its weapons sites to ensure that all the missiles had been removed. Castro refused to permit the inspectors to enter Cuba. Instead, the missiles were lashed to the decks of Soviet ships, and an American aircraft photographed them from above. President Kennedy made no vigorous effort to force the inspection issue.

On November 9, 1962, the final two ships removing Soviet missiles departed Cuba. Each ship was inspected at sea by US naval ships. Canvas covers were pulled off the missile transporters and the contents were photographed. This image shows the Soviet ship *Bratek* with two uncovered missiles on deck.

The Unswerving Objective

For his part, Nikita Khrushchev told the world he had won a victory in Cuba. He devoted only a short chapter of his memoirs to the Cuban Missile Crisis, referred to as the Caribbean Crisis in that country. The Soviet leader said he put the missiles in Cuba in order to safeguard that island nation from a US invasion. He now had a pledge from the United States not to invade. Therefore, the missiles had served their purpose and were no longer needed.

Several American generals were upset with the Cuban settlement. They believed the Soviets were hiding missiles somewhere on Cuban soil. Other military officials had wanted to invade Cuba in order to stamp out a Communist government operating so close to US shores. Angriest of all was the US Air Force chief Curtis E. LeMay. Banging his hand on a table, LeMay said the settlement was "the greatest defeat in our history." He shouted at Kennedy, "We should invade today!"[2]

President Kennedy was shocked by LeMay's outburst. He later remarked to Robert McNamara that he felt a closeness with Khrushchev because the Soviet leader probably had "to cope with a Curtis LeMay of his own."[3]

The American people felt a sense of relief and victory after the missiles were taken away. All apparent signs said the Soviets backed down under the US threat of force. The promise to remove missiles from Turkey and Italy was not made public. The US pledge not to invade Cuba was announced, but that was a minor concession. Most Americans believed their country faced the crisis bravely. Peace prevailed.

U-2 aircraft continued to fly over Cuba surveying the now-vacated missile sites. The Cuban army had antiaircraft guns, but it could not hit the high-flying planes. Soviet forces, armed with antiaircraft missiles, could have knocked down the U-2s. But the Soviets were under orders from Moscow not to fire at the American airplanes.[4] President Kennedy held a news conference on December 10, 1962. He told reporters that U-2 photos and other intelligence indicated all Soviet offensive missiles and bombers had been withdrawn from Cuba. Now it was official. The Cuban Missile Crisis had come to an end.

Cuba and the United States Today

US president Barack Obama and Cuban president Raúl Castro made great strides to establish a normal relationship between the United States and Cuba. They worked together to restore

diplomatic ties and ease travel restrictions. Since restoring relations in 2015 and up until June 2018, officials from the United States and Cuba have held seven Bilateral Commission meetings. At the meetings, officials have negotiated bilateral agreements on issues ranging from environmental cooperation to cancer research to the defining the limits of of the United States–Cuban maritime boundary in the eastern Gulf of Mexico.

President Donald Trump and Cuban president Miguel Diaz-Canel have not had the same relationship as their respective predecessors. President Trump reimposed restrictions on tourism for US citizens. He also prohibited trade with Cuban businesses owned by the military and intelligence services.

President Obama (*right*) and President Castro shake hands at a bilateral meeting that took place September 29, 2015, in New York City. US Secretary of State John Kerry (*bottom right*) smiles at the gesture.

Peace and Power

The Cuban Missile Crisis brought the world closer to nuclear annihilation than it had ever been before. For thirteen days, the fate of the world rested in a delicate balance. Frighteningly, a catastrophic war could have broken out despite the efforts of the American and Soviet leaders to stop the violence. Neither side wanted to see world tension reach such perilous heights again.

The confrontation between the two nuclear superpowers and the fear it generated throughout the world ushered in a major thaw in the Cold War. On June 10, 1963, eight months after the crisis, President Kennedy gave a speech to the graduating class of American University in Washington, DC. The president told the graduates: "I speak of peace . . . in an age when a single nuclear weapon contains almost ten times the explosive force delivered by all the allied air forces in the Second World War . . . an age when the deadly poisons produced by a nuclear exchange would be carried by wind and water and soil and seed to the far corners of the globe and to generations yet unborn. . . ."[5]

President Kennedy urged Americans to take a fresh view of their rival nation. He said: "Let us reexamine our attitude toward the Soviet Union. . . . In the final analysis, our most basic common link is that we all inhabit this small planet. We all breathe the same air. We all cherish our children's future. And we are all mortal. . . . Our problems are man-made—therefore, they can be solved by man.[6]

Still speaking to the graduates, Kennedy announced the United States would not begin a new round of atomic-bomb tests that were scheduled to take place in the atmosphere. Such aboveground tests poison the air. He also said Soviet,

British, and American negotiators would soon meet to discuss a treaty banning all atmospheric nuclear testing.

The Limited Test Ban Treaty took effect later in 1963. Though the ban did not have much practical effect on the development of nuclear weapons, the terms of the treaty did establish an important precedent for future

The Nuclear Football

After the Cuban Missile Crisis, it was determined an effective command system was needed in order to maintain a reliable nuclear deterrent. The United States decided on a briefcase officially known as the Presidential Emergency Satchel. This briefcase allows the president to order a nuclear attack within minutes.

When the president is at the White House, the briefcase remains in the Situation Room. When he is away, the briefcase, referred to as the "football," goes where he goes. A military aide who follows a few steps behind the president carries it. The modified aluminum briefcase is wrapped in black leather and weighs 45 pounds (20 kg) when filled.

The football does not contain a nuclear button nor can the president launch a strike directly from the briefcase. Once opened, the contents can be used to verify the identity of the president, communicate with the National Military Command Center in the Pentagon, and provide a list of strike options.

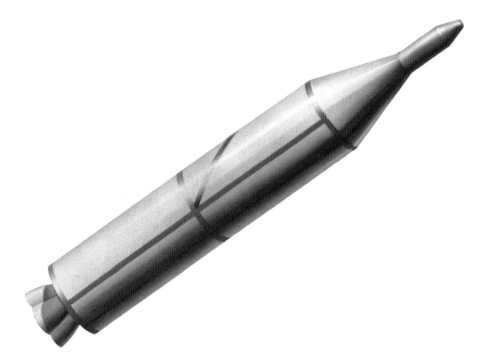

The first successful test launch of the Polaris submarine launched ballistic missile (SLBM) occurred on January 7, 1960, from a facility in Cape Canaveral, Florida. The Polaris was designed to hit a target about 1,500 miles (2,400 km) away.

arms control. The treaty was signed by the United States, the USSR, and Great Britain. It banned all nuclear tests in the atmosphere, in space, and underwater. Underground testing was still permitted. The Non-Proliferation Treaty (1968), the Strategic Arms Limitation Talks (SALT) agreements (1972), and the Threshold Test Ban Treaty (1974) followed the Limited Test Ban Treaty.

In August 1963, the United States and the Soviet Union installed a "hotline," which connected Moscow and Washington. During the Cuban Missile Crisis, it took hours for the two leaders to exchange letters through cablegrams. Now there was a direct telephone line between Washington and Moscow. It was hoped the hotline telephone connection could prevent accidental nuclear war.

Despite the Cold War thaw, the arms race continued at its old blistering pace. Polaris missiles housed in submarines that patrolled the Mediterranean Sea replaced the US missiles withdrawn from Turkey. The Soviet Union concentrated its efforts on building ICBMs. The ICBMs, based on Soviet soil, could hit targets in the United States. By the end of the 1960s, the Soviets had more ICBMs than did the Americans.[7] The United States, in turn, developed a method of putting several warheads on one missile. Despite the implications of the Cuban Missile Crisis, nuclear missiles continued to be a tool in the world's arsenal of weapons.

CONCLUSION

While much was learned from the Cuban Missile Crisis and its aftermath, a nuclear threat still exists in the world. The arms race is alive and well with every nuclear armed country developing new weapons.

During the Cold War, the United States government provided its citizens with information to prepare for a nuclear attack, and the same is true today. The nation's Department of Homeland Security supports a website, www.ready.gov. The site provides pertinent information related to preparation for natural disasters, such as hurricanes, floods, and earthquakes. It also has links to nuclear explosion, bioterrorism, and radiological dispersion device preparedness.

Russia remains a nuclear weapons powerhouse, but it is not the only country that concerns the United States. Other countries, such as North Korea and Iran, also pose a serious risk. Russian president Vladimir Putin has also warned that there still exists a real threat of nuclear war. He acknowledges that if nuclear war happened, it could lead to the collapse of civilization and possibly the entire planet.

On July 4, 2017, North Korea announced that it had successfully tested its first intercontinental ballistic missile. North Korean leader Kim Jong-un (*second from bottom right*) oversaw the test-fire. The missile reached an altitude of 1,730 miles (2,784 km) and flew horizontally about 575 miles (925 km) before falling into the Sea of Japan.

Despite the continued threat, treaties that were designed to control the world's nuclear forces are losing ground. US President Ronald Reagan and Soviet General Secretary Mikhail Gorbachev originally signed the Intermediate

Nuclear Forces Treaty (INF) in 1987. The purpose of the treaty was to reduce the risk of catastrophic war and strengthen international peace and security by eliminating intermediate-range and shorter-range missiles. Recently, government leaders in the US have indicated that it may withdraw from the treaty because of the belief that some countries may be violating the terms of the treaty.

There is also the possibility that the New Strategic Arms Reduction Treaty (New START) signed in April 2010 may not be extended. New START's purpose is to reduce nuclear arsenals. The initial duration of the treaty was ten years with the ability to extend it for an additional five years. In February 2018, both Russia and the United States announced that New START limitations had been met. The parties do have the option to withdraw from the treaty if certain extraordinary events jeopardize a country's supreme interests. If both the INF Treaty and New START are no longer in place, nuclear forces in Russia and the United States will have no constraints for the first time since 1972.

At the Havana Conference in January 1992, Robert McNamara, who played a crucial role in the Cuban Missile Crisis, acknowledged just how close the United States came to a nuclear war in 1962. In fact, as the Havana Conference drew to a close, he stated that the danger was actually greater than the public thought and more severe than even he believed. His words to the conference attendees still ring true: "This is simply another example that human beings are incapable of fully controlling such complex situations as military conflict among nations today. Now, that is dangerous in a world equipped with conventional weapons. It is absolutely potentially disastrous in a world that has as many nuclear weapons as we have today."[1]

CHRONOLOGY

1959 On New Year's Day, Fidel Castro and his followers take over Cuba.

1960 On May 1, an American U-2 spy plane is shot down over Soviet territory triggering heightened Cold War tension between the two countries.

1961 On April 17, anti-Castro Cuban exiles invade Cuban shores at the Bay of Pigs. The operation is supported by the United States and it fails, resulting in the death or capture of the exiles.

1962 In July, Fidel Castro's brother Raúl, visits the Soviet Union where the Soviet leader, Nikita Khrushchev, secretly offers to put missiles on Cuban soil. The Castro government accepts the offer.

October 14: An American U-2 spy plane captures photographs of fields in Cuba being cleared by workers. Experts conclude the fields will house missile launchers.

October 16: A group of Kennedy advisers, a team that will soon be called ExComm, meet to discuss what can be done about the Soviet missiles being installed in Cuba.

October 17: With President Kennedy in Connecticut, ExComm members ponder two possible moves against the missiles: a naval blockade or an air strike. Either could lead to nuclear war with the USSR.

October 18: Members of ExComm are dividing into "hawks," who favor aggressive action, and "doves," who wish to negotiate with the Soviets.

October 19: ExComm recommends a naval blockade, which will be referred to as a quarantine, of Cuba.

October 20: President Kennedy is in Chicago when it is announced he has a cold and will have to return to Washington to recover. Journalists suspect there is a crisis somewhere in the world.

October 21: US armed forces are put on high alert.

October 22: President Kennedy makes a speech to the nation announcing the quarantine. In strong language, he urges Khrushchev to withdraw the missiles from Cuba.

October 23: Cuba is surrounded by US naval ships, and fear grips the United States.

October 24: Most—but not all—Soviet ships stop before they reach the American quarantine line.

October 25: The first intercept takes place between Soviet and American vessels with no incidents, while in the United Nations, Ambassador Adlai Stevenson and Soviet delegate Valerian Zorin have a heated exchange.

October 26: Journalist John Scali receives a telephone call from Soviet operative Aleksandr Fomin asking if the United States would pledge not to invade Cuba in exchange for a Soviet withdrawal of the missiles. Later, a letter from Khrushchev poses the same question.

October 27: A US destroyer confronts a submarine armed with a nuclear torpedo; U-2 pilot Major Rudolf Anderson is shot down and killed over Cuba becoming the only casualty of the missile crisis; Khrushchev sends a second letter to Kennedy, this time demanding the United States remove its missiles from Turkey. Kennedy responds, ignoring the missile trade-off demand.

October 28: Khrushchev announces he is removing the missiles in exchange for an American pledge not to invade Cuba. In a private agreement, the United States said it will soon take its missiles out of Turkey. The Cuban Missile Crisis is over.

1963 The United States and the USSR agree to stop testing nuclear weapons everywhere except underground with the signing of the Partial Nuclear Test Ban Treaty; President John F. Kennedy is assassinated in Dallas, Texas, on November 22.

1964 Nikita Khrushchev is removed from power in the USSR in part for perceived failures during the Cuban Missile Crisis.

1968 Robert F. Kennedy is assassinated in California on June 6.

1970 An international treaty, the Nuclear Non-Proliferation Treaty, is negotiated to prevent the spread of nuclear weapons.

1971 Nikita Khrushchev dies of a heart attack on September 11.

1989 The Berlin Wall is demolished, reunifying East and West Berlin.

1991 The USSR is dissolved and becomes independent countries, marking the end of the Cold War.

2016 Fidel Castro dies of natural causes on November 25.

CHAPTER NOTES

Introduction

1. Kyle Mizokami, "Pentagon Confirms Existence of Russian Doomsday Torpedo," *Popular Mechanics*, January 16, 2018, https://www.popularmechanics.com/military/weapons/a15227656/pentagon-document-confirms-existence-of-russian-doomsday-torpedo/.
2. Kristin Houser, "US Report Confirms Russia Is Developing the World's Most Powerful Nuclear Weapon: The 100-megaton Thermonuclear Weapon Isn't 'Fake News,'" Futurism, January 30, 2018, https://futurism.com/us-report-confirms-russia-developing-worlds-most-powerful-nuclear-weapon.

CHAPTER 1
Unmistakable Evidence

1. Norman Polmar and John D. Gresham, *DEFCON-2* (Hoboken, NJ: John Wiley & Sons, 2006), p. 88.
2. Harold Evans, *The American Century* (New York, NY: Alfred A. Knopf, 2000), p. 492.
3. Don Munton and David A. Welch, *The Cuban Missile Crisis: A Concise History* (New York, NY: Oxford University Press, 2007), p. 48.

CHAPTER 2
A Difficult and Dangerous Time

1. "Korean War Fast Facts," CNN, updated April 30, 2018, https://www.cnn.com/2013/06/28/world/asia/korean-war-fast-facts/index.html.
2. History.com Editors, "Korean War," History, updated November 10, 2018, https://www.history.com/topics/korea/korean-war.

CHAPTER 3
An Atmosphere of Intimidation

1. "The Atomic Bombings of Hiroshima and Nagasaki: Total Casualties," Atomicarchive.com, http://www.atomicarchive

.com/Docs/MED/med_chp10.shtml (accessed February 13, 2019).

CHAPTER 4
Cuba: A Small Nation Makes an Enormous Difference in World Affairs

1. History.com Editors, "The USS Maine Explodes in Cuba's Harbor," History, updated February 15, 2019, https://www .history.com/this-day-in-history/the-maine-explodes.
2. Tad Szule, *Fidel: A Critical Portrait* (New York, NY: Harper Collins Publishers, 2000), p. 99.
3. James Eli Shiffer, "Annual Rent for Gitmo Naval Base: $4,085, Payable to Cuba," *Star Tribune,* October 10, 2014, http://www.startribune.com/annual-rent-for-gitmo-naval-base-4-085-payable-to-cuba/278810891/.
4. Szule, p. 100.
5. Aleksandr Fursenko and Timothy Naftali, *One Hell of a Gamble: The Secret History of the Cuban Missile Crisis, 1958–1964* (New York, NY: W. W. Norton & Co., 1997), p. 9.
6. Don Munton and David A. Welch, *The Cuban Missile Crisis: A Concise History* (New York, NY: Oxford University Press, 2007), p. 17.
7. Munton and Welch, p. 17.
8. Ernest R. May and Philip D. Zelikow, eds., *The Kennedy Tapes: Inside the White House During the Cuban Missile Crisis* (New York, NY: W.W. Norton & Company, 2002), p. 25.
9. May and Zelikow, p. 26.
10. Norman Polmar and John D. Gresham, *DEFCON-2* (Hoboken, NJ: John Wiley & Sons, 2006), p. 6.
11. Max Boot, "Operation Mongoose: The Story of America's Efforts to Overthrow Castro," *The Atlantic*, January 5, 2018, https://www.theatlantic.com/international/archive/2018/01/operation-mongoose/549737/.

CHAPTER 5

Clear and Present Danger

1. Norman Polmar and John D. Gresham, *DEFCON-2* (Hoboken, NJ: John Wiley & Sons, 2006), p. 16.
2. Thom Patterson, "JFK's 'Secret' Doomsday Map Revealed," CNN, April 12,2018, https://www.cnn.com/2018/04/06/ us/jfk-cuban-missile-crisis-map-auction/index.html.
3. Ernest R. May and Philip D. Zelikow, eds., *The Kennedy Tapes: Inside the White House During the Cuban Missile Crisis* (New York, NY: W.W. Norton & Company, 2002), p. 63.
4. Robert F. Kennedy, *Thirteen Days: A Memoir of the Cuban Missile Crisis* (New York, NY: W. W. Norton & Company, 1971), p. 28.
5. Nikita Khrushchev, trans., Strobe Talbott, *Nikita Khrushchev Remembers* (Boston, MA: Little Brown & Co., 1970), p. 493.
6. Richard Reeves, *President Kennedy: Profile of Power* (New York, NY: Simon and Schuster, 1993), p. 379.
7. Reeves, p. 379.
8. Reeves, p. 383.
9. Sheldon M. Stern, *The Week the World Stood Still: Inside the Secret Cuban Missile Crisis* (Stanford, CA: Stanford University Press, 2005), p. 69.
10. "Interdepartmental Cover Support to Operation Blue Moon," Central Intelligence Agency, https://www.cia. gov/library/readingroom/document/cia-rdp89b00569 r000900220046-2 (accessed January 10, 2019).

CHAPTER 6

The Abyss of Destruction

1. Norman Polmar and John D. Gresham, *DEFCON-2* (Hoboken, NJ: John Wiley & Sons, 2006), p. 121.
2. Robert F. Kennedy, *Thirteen Days: A Memoir of the Cuban Missile Crisis* (New York, NY: W. W. Norton & Company, 1971), p. 38.
3. Richard Reeves, *President Kennedy: Profile of Power* (New York, NY: Simon and Schuster, 1993), p. 391.

4. Aleksandr Fursenko and Timothy Naftali, *One Hell of a Gamble: The Secret History of the Cuban Missile Crisis, 1958–1964* (New York, NY: W. W. Norton & Co., 1997), p. 238.

5. Fursenko and Naftali, p. 238.

6. Reeves, p. 392.

7. "Historic Speeches," John F. Kennedy Presidential Library and Museum, https://www.jfklibrary.org/learn/about-jfk/historic-speeches/address-during-the-cuban-missile-crisis (accessed February 10, 2019).

CHAPTER 7
Continued and Increased Close Surveillance of Cuba

1. Russell Leadbetter, "Cuba Missile Crisis Day Eight: 'We Have Won a Considerable Victory. You are I are Still Alive,'" *The Herald*, October 23, 2017, https://www.heraldscotland.com/news/15610747.cuba-missile-crisis-day-eight-we-have-won-a-considerable-victory-you-and-i-are-still-alive/.

2. Norman Polmar and John D. Gresham, *DEFCON-2* (Hoboken, NJ: John Wiley & Sons, 2006), p. 139.

3. Polmar and Gresham, p. 135.

4. Richard Reeves, *President Kennedy: Profile of Power* (New York, NY: Simon and Schuster, 1993), p. 397.

5. Aleksandr Fursenko and Timothy Naftali, *One Hell of a Gamble: The Secret History of the Cuban Missile Crisis, 1958–1964* (New York, NY: W. W. Norton & Co., 1997), p. 256.

6. Robert F. Kennedy, *Thirteen Days: A Memoir of the Cuban Missile Crisis* (New York, NY: W. W. Norton & Company, 1971), p. 54.

7. Kennedy, p. 55.

8. Kennedy, p. 55.

9. Carole D. Bos, "Cuban Missile Crisis: Eyeball to Eyeball," Awesome Stories, updated February 15, 2016, https://www.awesomestories.com/asset/view/EYEBALL-TO-EYEBALL-Cuban-Missile-Crisis.

CHAPTER 8
Patience and Will Are Tested

1. Norman Polmar and John D. Gresham, *DEFCON-2* (Hoboken, NJ: John Wiley & Sons, 2006), p. 1.
2. Polmar and Gresham, p. 151.
3. Alice George, *Awaiting Armageddon: How Americans Faced the Cuban Missile Crisis* (Chapel Hill, NC: The University of North Carolina Press, 2003), p. xviii.
4. "Adlai Stevenson: UN Security Council Address on Soviet Missiles in Cuba," American Rhetoric, https://www.americanrhetoric.com/speeches/adlaistevensonunitednationscuba.html (accessed February 18, 2019).
5. Polmar and Gresham, p. 148.
6. George, p. 97.
7. Polmar and Gresham, p. 186.
8. Polmar and Gresham, p. 186.
9. Martin J. Sherman, "One Step from Nuclear War- The Cuban Missile Crisis at 50: In Search of Historical Perspective," National Archives, December 20, 2017, https://www.archives.gov/publications/prologue/2012/fall/cuban-missiles.html.
10. Robert F. Kennedy, *Thirteen Days: A Memoir of the Cuban Missile Crisis* (New York, NY: W. W. Norton & Company, 1971), p. 68.
11. George, p. xx.

CHAPTER 9
Force Shall Not Be Used

1. Norman Polmar and John D. Gresham, *DEFCON-2* (Hoboken, NJ: John Wiley & Sons, 2006), p. 162.
2. Casey Sherman and Michael J. Tougias, "War Was Avoided During the Cuban Missile Crisis, but One Man Died," History News Network, May 13, 2018, https://historynewsnetwork.org/article/168724.
3. Sherman and Tougias.
4. Polmar and Gresham, p. 163.

5. Sherman and Tougias.
6. Robert F. Kennedy, *Thirteen Days: A Memoir of the Cuban Missile Crisis* (New York, NY: W. W. Norton & Company, 1971), pp. 73–74.
7. Kennedy, p. 73.
8. Kennedy, p. 71.
9. Sheldon M. Stern, *The Week the World Stood Still: Inside the Secret Cuban Missile Crisis* (Stanford, CA: Stanford University Press, 2005), p. 186.
10. Alice George, *Awaiting Armageddon: How Americans Faced the Cuban Missile Crisis* (Chapel Hill, NC: The University of North Carolina Press, 2003), p. xxiii.
11. George, p. xxi.
12. Polmar and Gresham, p. 221.
13. Kennedy, p. 83.

CHAPTER 10

Peace and Security for All

1. Don Munton and David A. Welch, *The Cuban Missile Crisis: A Concise History* (New York, NY: Oxford University Press, 2007), p. 82.
2. Sheldon M. Stern, *The Week the World Stood Still: Inside the Secret Cuban Missile Crisis* (Stanford, CA: Stanford University Press, 2005), pp. 195–196.
3. Stern, p. 196.
4. Norman Polmar and John D. Gresham, *DEFCON-2* (Hoboken, NJ: John Wiley & Sons, 2006), p. 277.
5. "Commencement Address at American University," Atomic Archive, http://www.atomicarchive.com/Docs/Deterrence/Detente_JFK.shtml (accessed February 19, 2019).
6. "Commencement Address at American University."
7. Polmar and Gresham, p. 284.

Conclusion

1. James Blight, Bruce Allyn, and David Welch, *Cuba on the Brink: Castro, the Missile Crisis, and the Soviet Collapse* (New York, NY: Pantheon Books, 1993), p. 255.

GLOSSARY

arc A smooth curving line or movement.

ballistic missile A missile that is guided up into the atmosphere in a high arch, then free falls toward its target.

bilateral Involving two nations or other parties.

casualty A person killed or injured during a war.

Cold War A period from about 1945 to 1991 when the United States and the Soviet Union were locked in conflict, though the two nations never directly engaged in battle with one another.

covert Hidden or secret.

enclave An area or territory surrounded by another area or territory.

exile To be sent away from one's own country.

freeze In Cold War terms, a time of heightened tension between the capitalist and Communist worlds.

intercontinental Having the ability to travel between continents.

quarantine During the Cuban Missile Crisis, the word used instead of blockade to describe the US tactic to surround Cuba with US naval ships in order to intercept incoming vessels and prevent new missiles and crews from reaching the island.

reconnaissance A military mission to obtain information about an enemy force.

sieve In political terms, the word has been used to describe someone who habitually "leaks" information.

thaw Cold War language used to describe a period of relaxation and peace between the superpowers.

triad A group of three people or things often connected in some way.

FURTHER INFORMATION

BOOKS

Brimner, Larry Dane. *Blacklisted! Hollywood, the Cold War, and the First Amendment.* Honesdale, PA: Calkins Creek, 2018.

Bryan, Bethany. *The Bay of Pigs and the Cuban Missile Crisis.* New York, NY: Cavendish Square, 2017.

Duling, Kaitlyn. *Nuclear Proliferation, the Military-Industrial Complex, and the Arms Race.* New York, NY: Cavendish Square, 2017.

O'Reilly, Bill. *The Day the World Went Nuclear: Dropping the Atom Bomb and the End of World War II in the Pacific.* New York, NY: Henry Holt & Company, 2017.

Stone, Oliver, Peter Kuznick, and Eric Singer. *The Untold History of the United States, Volume 2: Young Readers Edition, 1945-1962.* New York, NY: Atheneum Books for Young Readers, 2019.

WEBSITES

Cuban Missile Crisis

www.cubanmissilecrisis.org/

Dive deeper into the Cuban Missile Crisis and check out original historic sources, photographs, and audio clips.

John F. Kennedy Presidential Library and Museum

www.jfklibrary.org/

Visit the archives to see and hear primary source materials, including photographs, audio recordings, and video clips that document the life, career, and times of John F. Kennedy.

Plan Ahead for Disasters

www.ready.gov/

Be prepared for any disaster—natural or man-made—with links that describe how to develop plans and prepare emergency kits for any situation.

FILMS

Cuban Missile Crisis: Three Men Go to War (2012), produced by John Murray.

The Fog of War: Eleven Lessons from the Life of Robert S. McNamara (2004), directed by Erroll Morris.

Thirteen Days (2005), directed by Roger Donaldson.

INDEX